W9-BTS-399

CATHY MALKASIAN

FANTAGRAPHICS BOOKS

EARTHA

Editor: Gary Groth
Designer: Keeli McCarthy
Production: Paul Baresh
Associate Publisher: Eric Reynolds
Publisher: Gary Groth

Fantagraphics Books, Inc.
7563 Lake City Way NE
Seattle, WA 98115

ISBN: 978-1-606999-912
Library of Congress Control Number: 2016947861
First Printing: March 2017
Printed in China

The author wishes to acknowledge:
My family and friends: thanks for putting up with all the shop talk!
And to the gang at Fantagraphics: you are stubborn and dedicated and uncompromising in all the right ways.

This story is dedicated to you, for taking the time to read it.

FALLOW

KEEP LOOKING!

STILL NOTHING.
YOU THINK THEY'RE GONE FOR GOOD?
CALM YOURSELF! IT'S BEEN ONLY A WEEK.
YAWN.
HEY DON'T YOU GO TAKING IT OUT ON MY GIRL!
EARTHA WHAT ARE YOU STANDING 'ROUND FOR?

IT'S ALL RIGHT, PAPA.
I'M JUST TIRED, IS ALL.
AAAHH-- NO HARM DONE.

?!
HOW LONG YOU THINK THIS'LL GO ON?
OH, LAD, I WISH I KNEW..

?.
??

FLOOD!!

GRAB A TREE AND HANG ON!!
?
WHAT'S GOING ON UP THERE?!

OH..
NOTHIN' MUCH.
JUST...
...THE USUAL.
AGAIN?!
??
WE'RE FINE NOW, TRULY.
ALL RIGHT.

RIGHT, THEN..
BACK TO IT...
YAWN.

EARTHA DEAR, I KNOW WHAT HAPPENED. IT'S YOUR MUM. SHE LEFT THE VALVE OPEN.

GO AND CHECK ON HER, WOULD YOU, LOVE?
AYE, PAPA.

TELL HER IT'S TIME SHE TOOK A REST!
AYE, PAPA.

MORNIN' EARTHA.
MORNIN'..
VALVE STATION

MAMA?

OVER HERE, EARTHA!

YOUR MUM WAS CHECKING THE VALVES, THEN SHE JUST RAN OFF.

THE TURNIP FIELD FLOODED.
AYE, AND IT WOULD'VE EVEN MORE HAD I NOT SHUT THE VALVE WITH MY HORNS! NOT EASY...

GO AND CHECK ON HER, WOULD YOU, DEAR? SHE IS BEHAVING MOST ODDLY TODAY.

I MIGHT'VE HEARD HER CRYING!

SHE'S A LAUGHER, NOT A CRIER!

HA, HA!

MAMA?

OH HA HA!

AHHH! HA, HA, HA, WEE HA!
HA!

?
EARTHA, DO YOU SEE IT?

SEE WHAT, MAMA?

THAT!!

THERE!

UH... OH-- IT'S GONE.

SHE'S BEEN EATING THE PLUMS AGAIN!
HALLUCINATING!
DRUNK!
AHHHH! LISTEN TO YOU BUNCH OF BUSYBODIES!

THE TREE'S NEVER FRUITED BEFORE! TEN PLUMS IS ALL I'VE HAD!

EARTHA, LOOK AT THIS PIT...

...A BIT OF WHAT WAS, A BIT OF WHAT'S TO COME. PAST AND FUTURE, PERFECTLY ENCASED IN DARKNESS.

MAMA, YOU'RE TIRED.
'COURSE I AM!

AREN'T YOU COLD UP HERE?
NO, MAMA. DID YOU KNOW THAT YOU FLOODED THE TURNIP FIELD?
DID I?

WAS IT BAD?
AYE.

UP TO PAPA'S KNEES?
NO--HIS WAIST, BUT I GRABBED HIM IN TIME.

HA HA
HA HA
HA HA
HA..

HE'S SO, SO ORGANIZED! THE LEAST MISHAP THROWS HIM.

WHAT SHOULD I TELL HIM?

THE TRUTH, OF COURSE! THAT I WAS CHECKING THE VALVES AND THE FIELD LEVELS...

...I'D HAD ME A FEW OF THOSE PLUMS, WHEN I SAW A BRIGHT AND BEAUTIFUL VISION.
NO WORDS FOR IT..

AND NOW, WELL, ALL'S I GOT LEFT IS THIS FEELIN'...

CALL IT A "BACKWARDS NOSTALGIA," HA, HA...

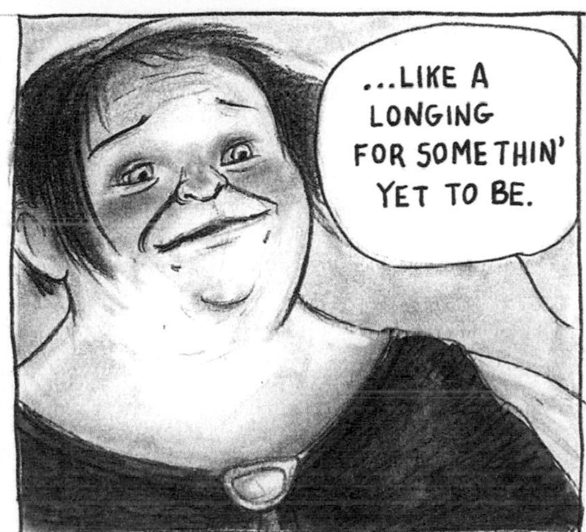
...LIKE A LONGING FOR SOMETHIN' YET TO BE.

TELL ME-- HAVE THEY FOUND ANY DREAMS DOWN THERE?
NOT A ONE, MAMA.

A WHOLE WEEK WITHOUT DREAMS. IT GETS ME WORRIED.
AYE, HA, HEH... 'TIS A SILLY THING, WHEN YOU THINK ON IT.

I'M TIRED OF WORRYING. NOW GIVE US A HUG.
THAT'S MY GIRL! HA, HA.

KEEP PAPA BUSY! I'LL BE DOWN SOON.

PAPA?

I COULDN'T WAIT.

SHE'S FINE, PAPA, JUST TIRED.
OH, THANK THE STARS! THAT WOMAN WILL BE THE DEATH OF ME YET...

SHE GOT INTO THOSE PLUMS AGAIN, DIDN'T SHE?
AYE, PAPA.
THEY MAKE HER DAFFY! SHE SHOULD LEAVE THE REST FOR THE BUFFALO.
AYE, PAPA.

NOW DON'T YOU DARE TELL YOUR MA THAT I WAS WORRYING! SHE'LL JUST LAUGH ALL THE MORE!
BUT--OH, HOW I LOVE THAT LAUGH OF HERS!
CALMS ME RIGHT DOWN.

THAT WIFE OF MINE...

WHAT DOES SHE FIND SO FUNNY?

EVERYTHING, APPARENTLY...

AND YOU'RE JUST LIKE HER, EARTHA...

...NEVER TAKING A WORRY TILL YOU NEED IT.

MIND YOU, THE BAKERS NEED THAT FLOUR.
AYE, PAPA.

There were many constants in Echo Fjord: the oblong sun, the harvests and tides... ...and Eartha.
Big as a boulder and softer than the moss that grew on it, Eartha was everyone's friend.

Everyone enjoyed her company, though she said very little.

Like the land they loved, folks in Echo Fjord were well-furrowed and open. They plowed and picked and hauled every food that grew from darkness. For them, night was underground, and it met the day in a promising shoot.

DID YA KNOW THAT EVERY SQUID CAN COUNT UP TO TEN THOUSAND?

YOU DON'T SAY!..

Eartha was more open than most. If any fool made a confident claim then she believed him.

She'd defend even the most drunken conviction because she admired the weight of it, and she enjoyed the smiles of those who thought they'd been believed.

ALL TRUE, ALL TRUE, ALL...

ZZ

When Maybelle was near her Eartha felt safe. When she was not, Eartha took to wondering if her substance would scatter to the winds.

Such musings rattled her. She kept them away from friendly conversation...
MAYBELLE?

...often hardly saying a word...
...which was fine, since most folk brought their own chatter with them...

...and had their many chores to do.
WHERE IS MAYBELLE?

THERE YOU ARE!
WHERE ELSE WOULD I BE?!
It seemed there'd never been a time without Maybelle. Since they were children they'd argued everything and felt smarter for it. Other times they'd speak without speaking. Their love was sure, and Eartha felt fearless around her.

EARTHA'S BROUGHT THE FLOUR!
EARTHA!
BAKE

EARTHA, WOULD YA' TAKE THESE STICKY BUNS TO YOUR FOLKS?
AYE.

ANY NEW DREAMS IN THE FIELDS?
NAY.

WHO'S THE KING NOW?!

ME!

ME!!! I AM THE KING!

DREAM!

A DREAM!
PHEW-- I'VE BEEN FOLLOWING THIS ONE FOR MILES.
WHERE'D YOU FIND IT, FRANK?
IN THE BEET FIELDS?

NO--BY THE YAM SLOPES. OH, I NEED A REST!
I'LL TAKE IT OFF YOUR HANDS.

The Fjord grew many crops, and most stayed put till picked...
...except the **Dreams**...
LOOK AT HIM GO!

Echo Fjord had long been a refuge for escaped dreams. They journeyed there from the City Across the Sea.
AH-- LOOK!
The city Dreams were lively and entertaining wisps of thought.

Each one of them was a wonder to behold: glowing from within, it sported a bright shaft of light from its head.
That light could be seen for miles.

City dreams came to Echo Fjord for one reason: to finish the stories of their lives.
HE'S A LIVE ONE!
HURRY, EARTHA!

City minds were crowded places, waking and sleeping.
Filled with unquenched yearnings and shames, they had little room for dreams.

Daydreams, night dreams--they all knew when they were not wanted.

Any distraction could set a dream adrift...

...and off it went to sea.
This was a longstanding custom.

The sea took in all dreams, letting them drive its currents to the faraway Fjord.

This had been the way of things for a thousand years, from the time the city was born.
Its new inhabitants had always lived in wide open spaces, where dreams could roam and float freely, away from their dreamers.
They haunted the city, airing secret hatreds, plots and longings. The city grime weighed them down and kept them from floating away.
Confined within City walls, dreams had nowhere to wander but under everyone's noses. They said and did unmentionable things, causing rifts and disruptions in every home and institution.
#@&!!
!!
City leaders panicked-- what to do with this plague of shames?
The answer came by sea...

The Dreams took to the Fjord instantly, attaining their wishes, then dissolving into thin air. The City was rid of its pestilence and the Fjord became the livliest of places, its folk contentedly shepherding the desires of strangers. Dreams were a steady influx of unvarnished news, not so much a chronicle of city events as a ruminative reaction to them, with worries and hopes embodied in lavish variety.

And so it went: Fjord traders stayed away from the City Across the Sea, and it got on with its business, ignorant of the fate of its banished Dreams. In very little time the Fjord disappeared from city maps and minds, and the City all but disappeared to the Fjord.
Except, of course, for the occasional..
DREAM!
LOOK, EARTHA, ANOTHER ONE!

LOOK AT THAT LIGHT!

THAT'S TWO DREAMS WE'VE SEEN. YOU THINK THE FALLOW'S OVER?
NAY. WE NEED TO SEE THOUSANDS.
LOOK AT HIM...
SOME KIND OF OFFICIAL..
HE'S IN A HURRY!
AYE...
I CAN'T HOLD HIM FOR MUCH LONGER!
I'LL PUT ON THE SHADOW.

Dreams that had traveled across the sea needed a boost of energy to ignite them back into themselves.

ONWARD, MEN!
EARTHA! MAYBELLE!
THIS ONE'S LEADING SOME KINDA ARMY!
YOU THINK THERE'S A WAR IN THE CITY?
COULDN'T SAY...
OURS IS SAYING HE'S A KING...
...BUT HE'S REALLY A ROOSTER!
WELL, WELL, WELL...

MAYBELLE..
MMM?

THERE USED TO BE THOUSANDS OF DREAMS...

DON'T PANIC, LOVE. KEEP YOUR EYES ON THE DREAMS WE'VE GOT.

WHAT'S HE DOING?
AH!

TOUCH MY FACE AND YOU'LL SEE WHAT I'M SEEIN'...

?!!?

CLUCK, CLUCK, PICK ME! CLUCK...
PICK ME!!
WELL, WELL..
NO-- PICK ME!
CLUCK
CLUCK, CLUCK!
PICK ME!

I'VE HEARD ABOUT THIS ONE-- ALWAYS THE SAME STORY!-- BUT I'VE NEVER GUIDED IT TILL NOW...

WHO'S THE KING?
OOOH...
YOU ARE!!

YOU THINK IT'S A SEX DREAM?
AYE. THEY NEVER MAKE MUCH SENSE..

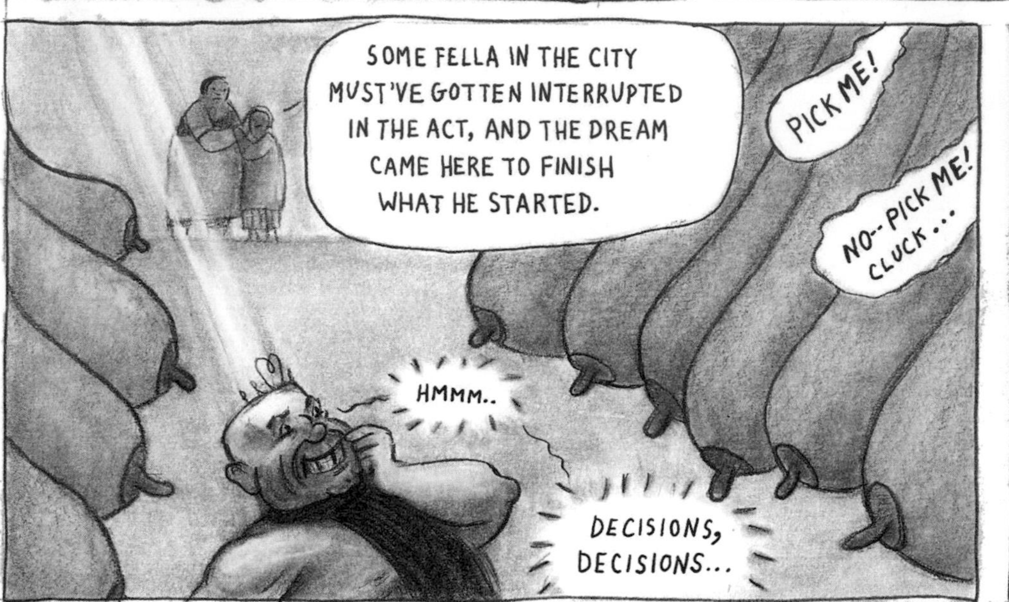
SOME FELLA IN THE CITY MUST'VE GOTTEN INTERRUPTED IN THE ACT, AND THE DREAM CAME HERE TO FINISH WHAT HE STARTED.
PICK ME!
NO-- PICK ME! CLUCK...
HMMM..
DECISIONS, DECISIONS...

IT PROBABLY CAME FROM A "ONE-HANDED ROMANCER"...
!
!
YOU!
CLUCK!
CLUCK!
HMMM.. HAVING HIS FUN ALL ALONE..

WHATEVER THE CASE...

...IT'LL BE QUICK.
AREN'T YOU SUCCULENT...
...AND.. SAVORY..
OOOOOOHH! SO FORBIDDEN..

CLUCK!
CLUCK!
CLUCK!
AAGGGHHH!

I DON'T EVEN HAVE TO GUIDE HIM! THESE REPEAT CUSTOMERS SHOW THEMSELVES OUT.

MAYBELLE?
HMMM?
IT'S SO QUIET NOW, SO... LONELY HERE...

WHERE DID THE DREAMS GO?

OH LOVE! LOOK AT ME...
DREAM DEPARTURES

OUR LIFE'S ABOUT BEING TOGETHER, AND FINDING JOY IN THE THINGS WE CAN'T EXPLAIN!

NOW LET'S CATCH UP TO THAT DREAM...

AHH! THERE HE IS..

AND OFF HE GOES.

I ALWAYS ENJOY THIS PART.

WATCHING THEM DISSOLVE...
...THEN SWEEPING UP THEIR SHADOWS.

EVEN THE TRIVIAL ONES ARE A WONDER.

I NEVER REALIZED HOW MUCH WE NEED THEM.

THEY'LL BE BACK, EARTHA.

WILL YOU GO DANCING WITH ME TONIGHT?
AYE, LOVE.

SEE YOU THEN.

THAT YOU, EARTHA?
AYE, EARL.
MORNIN', CHAZ.
MORNIN', EARTHA.
SHADOW

YOU HAVE ROOM FOR MORE?
TOO MUCH ROOM THESE DAYS..

I MAY BE BLIND, BUT I SEE WHAT'S GOING ON HERE: WE'RE DOWN TO OUR LAST DREAMS!

FUNNY, AIN'T IT? WE'VE SEEN IT ALL, EVERY WISH AND HORROR IN THOSE DREAMS. I GUESS THAT MAKES US WORLDLY, EVEN THOUGH WE'VE ALWAYS STAYED PUT.
STEADY EARL, THERE'S BUMPS AHEAD.

CITY FOLK! TO THINK THE PEOPLE WE KNOW MOST INTIMATELY...

...DON'T EVEN KNOW WE EXIST.
SHADOW
EARL, WE'RE GOING DOWN..

EARTHA, YOU THINK OUR DREAMS GO ELSEWHERE, TOO?
NO, EARL.

MAMA SAYS OUR DREAMS DON'T HAVE TO GO ANYWHERE.
'CAUSE THEY'RE SATISFIED IN US.
WE'RE APPROACHING AN INCLINE, EARL.
SHADOW

SHE SAID WE'D FEEL IT IF OUR DREAMS SLIPPED OUT, LIKE CHILDREN RUNNING AWAY FROM HOME.

ZZZ
ZZ
ZZ
POOR CITY FOLK! TOO BUSY TO KNOW WHEN A DREAM'S RUN AWAY.
TWENTY MORE YARDS, EARL.
BARBER

I'M WORRIED FOR THEM.

ANY FOOL KNOWS THAT YOU CAN'T DREAM PROPERLY IF YOU DON'T FEEL **SAFE**.

MAYBE THE CITY IS JUST...*GONE*.
?
BYE, EARTHA.

What if the city was gone?

WELL LOOK WHO'S HERE!

No one had traveled to the City in a thousand years. No one even knew where it was.
IT'S ABOUT TIME!
EARTHA!

WILL IT BE HOPS TODAY, SWEETHEART?
AYE. THREE SACKS.

And yet everyone had come to rely on that invisible place and the dreams it sent.
Without them nothing felt certain...

City dreams had made the Fjord a grand place.
Now it felt small...

ZZZ

...And the people in it felt too big.
ZZZZ

SORRY, EARTHA... I WAS TOO MUCH IN THE PUB..
ZZ

GLORIA--I SAW TWO DREAMS THIS MORN'.
DIDJA NOW? WELL, MAYBE WE CAN GET BACK TO NORMAL.

zzZzz

EARTHA!

?

...ALL OF YOU! ATTENTION!
LISTEN TO HIM...

TO THE VAULTS, MEN, QUICKLY! TAKE WHATEVER SPOILS YOU CAN CARRY- A REWARD FOR YOUR ABSOLUTE ALLEGIANCE TO ME...

HE'S NOT MUCH OF A GENERAL, EARTHA.
BRAINLESS BASTARDS!
HE JUST LED HIS TROOPS INTO CHAMBERS OF TREASURES, LOCKED THEM IN AND GASSED THEM. ALL DEAD.

IT'S JUST A DREAM THOUGH, AIN'T IT?
I DON'T KNOW. COULD BE A PLAN...

SOMEBODY MIGHT BE FIXING TO BRING DOWN THE CITY.

ENTITLED SCUM!

AND YOU-- YES, YOU! I WILL CRUSH YOU FOR IGNORING ME!

I WILL KILL YOU WITH MY BARE HANDS!
JUST... SOME MAN'S DREAM.

AND BETTER HE DREAMS THE THING...
...THAN DOES IT...

MORNIN' EARTHA.

ANOTHER DREAM CAME IN BUT IT WENT STRAIGHT TO JUMPERS' BRIDGE.

MIND YOU-- IT'S A *FINAL* DREAM.

NO, **NO!**

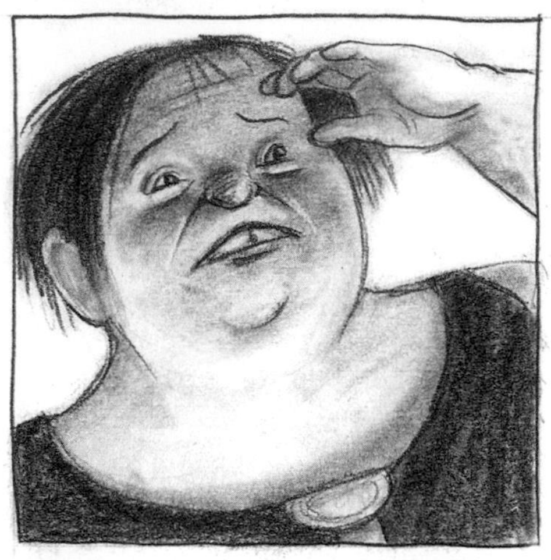

I AM *NOT A JUMPER!*

HE *PUSHED ME!!*

HE HAD NO RIGHT!
THE POOR DEAR.

HEY, EARTHA.
YOU ALL RIGHT?

YOU SEEN A JUMPER DREAM?
...AYE.
OH, THEY'RE ROUGH.

SHE DIDN'T WANT TO DIE..

GOIN' TO THE PUB?
AYE.
GIVE US A LIFT?

IT'S HARD, SEEING THOSE LAST MOMENT CHANGES OF HEART...
AYE.

JUMPER DREAMS WANT TO TAKE IT ALL BACK.
SEEIN' THEM FLY BACK UP-- OH!--IT'S TOO MUCH TO TAKE.

I SUPPOSE THAT ONE SAD DREAM IS BETTER THAN NONE THESE DAYS.
DON'T FRET, LAD.

THEY'LL SOON BE BACK IN DROVES.

WHAT DO YOU THINK, EARTHA?
?

WHERE'D SHE GO?

AH, EARTHA! WHAT WOULD THIS PUB DO WITHOUT YA?
YOU CAN LET GO, LOVE.
WE'VE GOT IT.
ZZZ

ZZZZZZ

HELLO, OSCAR.
ZZZZZZ

HA!
ZZZZ
RESTORING OSCAR'S DIGNITY.
HERE SHE IS!

I'LL SET HIM HERE.
OF COURSE, DARLIN'.
Z Z

NOW YOU SIT AND SOAK YOUR FEET WITH US.
Z Z Z

LAST WEEK I GUIDED THREE JACKASSES.
SO DID I...
STRANGE DREAMS THEY WERE.

BUT THIS WEEK? NOTHIN'.
NONE FOR ME, EITHER.

REMEMBER THE DREAM THAT WOULD REARRANGE THE STARS WITH A WAVE OF HER HAND?

HOW 'BOUT THE ONE THAT WOULD SIT ON A THRONE IN THE MIDDLE OF THE LAKE?
MMM..

REMEMBER WHEN THEY'D FLY?
YOU COULD BARELY HANG ONTO THEM BY THEIR SHADOWS!
Z Z
Z Z Z Z

HOW I MISS THE BLOOD FEUDS, THE EMBEZZLEMENTS, THE AFFAIRS!
OH, AND WHEN THEY'D FALL IN LOVE, OVER AN' OVER AGAIN...

EVERY YEAR ON THE SAME DAY I'D GET A DREAM PLOTTING HIS WIFE'S MURDER, THEN I'D GET THE WIFE'S DREAM PLOTTING *HIS!*
MUST'VE BEEN ON THEIR ANNIVERSARY...

WHAT ABOUT THE FIGHTER?
OH! SHE WAS GOOD.
ZZZ

SHE'D GATHER EVERY SOUL SHE'D EVER ARGUED WITH IN HER ENTIRE LIFE-- THOUSANDS, MIND YOU!-- AND THEY'D CHASE HER UP A CLIFF, SHOUTIN' INSULTS, THEN SHE'D HERD THEM ALL OVER THE EDGE, CACKLIN' WITH JOY!

OH, AND THE WAY THEY'D STARE RIGHT THROUGH YOU...
NOTHIN' LIKE A DREAM'S STARE.
ZZ

AND THEIR VOICES WHEN THEY'D SING WOULD RATTLE YOU JUST RIGHT.
?!
THOSE SONGS COULD SKITTER ACROSS THE LAKE AND SHATTER THE HILLS...
SUCH FINE TIMES.
ZZZ

LISTEN TO US! ONE WEEK OF FALLOW AND WE'VE GIVEN UP ON DREAMS! WHAT SAY YOU, EARTHA?
MAYBE... THEY JUST FOUND A NEW PLACE TO GO...

A NEW MIGRATION ROUTE? COULD BE.
NAH! I THINK THERE'S SOME KINDA WAR IN THE CITY.
ZZZ

WRONG! ALL *WRONG!*
ZZZ
YOUNG FOLK! WHAT DO *THEY* KNOW? HA, HEH...

NOW SOME SIXTY YEARS AGO THERE TRULY *WAS* A WAR OVER THERE, 'CAUSE THE DREAMS CAME TO THIS FJORD FILLED WITH MADNESS AND FRIGHT. FOR THREE STRAIGHT YEARS THAT'S HOW THEY WERE!

ALL THEIR WORRIES AN' WORST CASE SCENARIOS, PURE DREAD, AND SO VERY CRYSTAL CLEAR.
TYING UP LOOSE ENDS, THEY WERE.

BUT NOW--! THE DAYDREAMS, THE NIGHT DREAMS AREN'T BEING BIRTHED AT ALL! HOW CAN FOLKS NOT DREAM?
ZZZZ

ZZ
OH EARTHA, I CAN SEE IN THE MIRROR-- OUR BOY OSCAR...
IS HE TROUBLIN' YA'?

NOT AT ALL.
ZZZZ

THIS FJORD HAD A GOOD RUN FOR A THOUSAND YEARS.
PERHAPS THIS EMPTINESS IS OUR BETTER FATE.

ZZZZ
I JUST FEAR FOR OUR OSCAR! HOW HE USED TO LOVE CHASIN' THOSE DREAMS AROUND.

I'LL GO TO THE CITY, PAPA! I'LL FIND OUT WHAT IS AMISS!

OH NO YOU WON'T! NOBODY'S MADE THAT TRIP IN AGES!
IT AIN'T POSSIBLE!

ALL RIGHT, THEN.. ZZZ
THAT'S OUR BOY!
KEEP THE ALE COMIN' AN' HE'LL SEE DREAMS AGAIN.
HA.

THERE YOU ARE!
WE LOOKED IN ALL THE WRONG PLACES..

STILL THINKIN' ABOUT THAT JUMPER?
AYE.

MIND YOU, I'VE SEEN MY SHARE OF FINAL DREAMS...
MM--THE DEATHBED BROODINGS..

ALL THOSE SECRETS THE CITY FOLK TAKE TO THE GRAVE! THEY COME HERE AND HAVE A VERY PLEASANT TIME.

BUT THERE HAVE BEEN ONLY A FEW OF LATE, NOTHING OF NOTE...
SO DON'T FRET OVER CITY AFFAIRS! THEY'LL STRAIGHTEN OUT.

ODDS ARE THE CITY'S FINE.
YEP.

PAPA SAYS THAT EVERY TIME A DREAM LEAVES HERE SATISFIED...

...SOMEWHERE IN THE CITY A DREAMER FEELS LIGHTER.

AN' THEY WILL AGAIN!

YOU'D BETTER GO HELP YOUR PAPA. I HEAR HE'S WEARING HIMSELF OUT.

HMMM--THAT'S MAMA'S BOAT...

EARTHA!

YER MAMA'S OVER THERE, FIGHTIN' WITH YER PAPA!

YOU THINK IT'S A **DREAM** THEY'RE FIGHTIN' OVER?

I DON'T KNOW, BUT THEY BOTH NEED A REST.

HA! SOME DREAM HUNTER YOU ARE!

GO TAKE A NAP BEFORE YOU FALL OVER!
HA HA!!
DON'T YOU TELL ME --*YAWN*-- WHAT TO DO!
YAWN

HAS ANYONE CHECKED THE CAVES? *NO!* THEY COULD BE SPROUTING UP IN THERE AS WE SPEAK!

EARTHA, TALK SOME SENSE INTO YER FATHER! HE WON'T LISTEN TO ME.
ZZZ

HA--
LOOK!

WHAT A LIGHT FROM THAT HEAD!
MUST BE A CHILD'S..

THIS ONE'S NEW...
YOU WANT TO GUIDE IT?
AYE, PAPA.

THESE CHILDREN'S DREAMS ARE LIVE ONES--IN A HURRY...

ELEGANT WORK, YOU TWO.
S

LOOK AT HER!
GIVE HER YOUR PULSE, LOVE!

GO, LOVE, GO!
!!!
!
?
!

A DREAM PARK...
...FOR A CHILD..

MOON.

?
MOON!

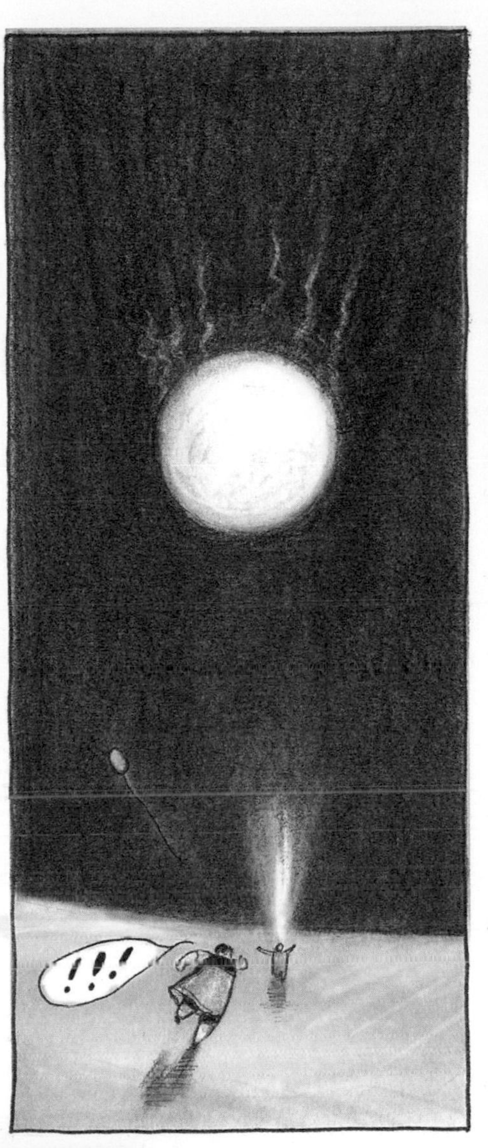

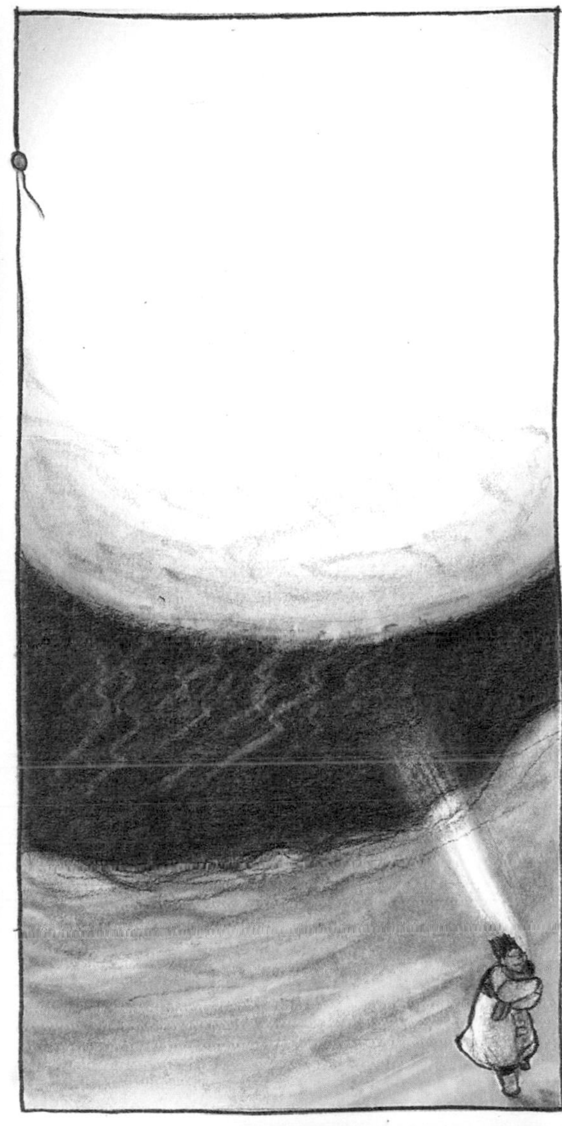

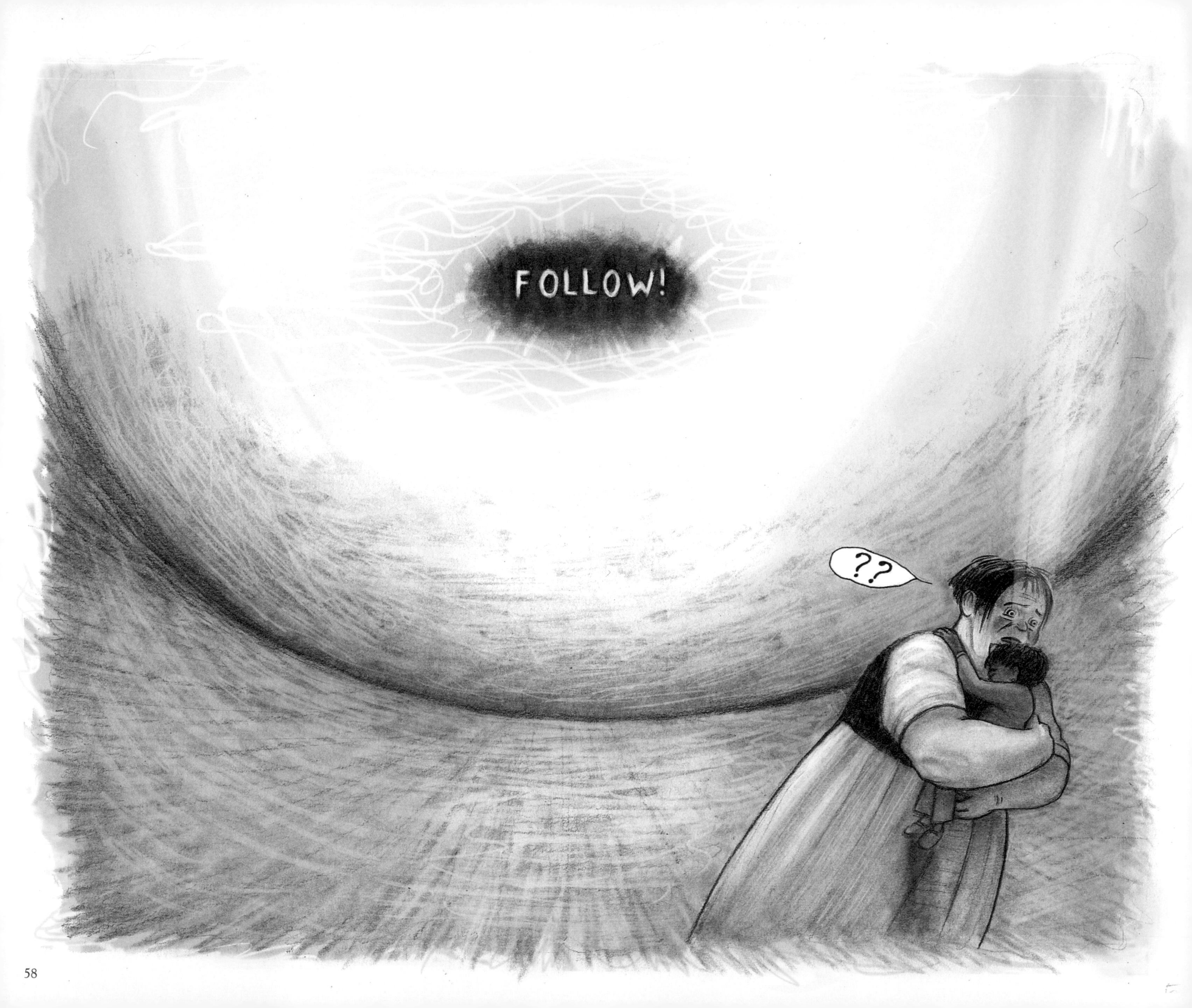
FOLLOW!
??

EARTHA?

WHAT WERE YOU RUNNING FROM?

YOU WANT ME TO SCRAPE OFF THE SHADOW?

WAS IT A GOOD DREAM?

I DON'T KNOW...

I SAW A MOON FALL TO THE GROUND.
A CHILD'S NIGHTMARE, IS ALL...
JUST ONE MORE BAD DREAM..

OH DARLIN'..
WHAT IF THE MOON CRUSHED THE CITY?

WE ALL NEED A REST! LET OUR OWN DREAMS LIVE!
HA! FOR ONCE PAPA AND I AGREE.
ZZZ ZZ

LET'S FACE IT! WE'RE ALL WORN OUT.
'TIS TRUE.

WAITIN' FOR OTHER FOLKS' DREAMS!
YAWN..
HA, HA, HA! A TOO FUNNY THING, WHEN YOU THINK ABOUT IT.

ZZZZZ

MAKE A RECORD OF IT, LOVE.
AYE, PAPA.

HMMM--AN UNUSUAL ONE. I'VE NEVER HEARD OF IT.

HAS A MOON EVER FALLEN IN THE CITY?
NOT THAT ANYONE'S DREAMED.

HERE'S YOURS AND ALL OF YESTERDAY'S RECORDS. A PALTRY FEW, BUT NONETHELESS THEY MUST BE RECORDED AND ARCHIVED. TAKE 'EM UP TO OLD LLOYD, DEAR.

STAY UP AT THE ARCHIVES, DO WHATEVER YOU WANT, BUT TAKE THE REST OF THIS DAY OFF, Y'HEAR?

BUT PAPA, I NEED TO KEEP BUSY...
AND YOU WILL...

TOMORROW!

Echo Fjord had always relied on City Dreams to help them tell the time and sense the wider world.
Now no one could feel what to do or where to go.
Knowing no other way, Echo Fjord simply kept going.

But Eartha had questions...
TO ARCHIVE

ARCHIVE
...and only one place in the Fjord had answers.

OLD LLOYD?
The Archivists were Echo Fjord's master cataloguers. Purveyors of inner histories, they collected and arranged records of every Dream that had ever visited the Fjord.
OLD LLOYD? OLD LLOYD??
No one knew more secrets, patterns and cycles than the Archivists. They preserved all Dream histories in quiet, cavernous halls.

Old Lloyd was Eartha's closest friend and the oldest, most cantankerous resident of Echo Fjord. As Senior Archivist, he knew every Dream story printed on every scroll.

THIS TOO IS JUNK!!!

SONOFABITCH...

MY HERNIA BELT IS KILLING ME AND NOW THEY MAKE ME STEP OUTSIDE TO SPIT.

NOT ONCE IN MY EIGHTY YEAR TENURE HAVE I EVER SPAT ON A SCROLL. I'M A NATURALLY CLEAN PERSON!

YOU'RE TRYING TO KILL ME!!
NOT SO, OLD LLOYD.

WHAT AM I, A LEPER?? SIT.

TELL ME-- HOW IS YOUR MOTHER? SHE MAKES ME LAUGH.

WELL, TODAY SHE--
OH, TERRIFIC!!!

ANOTHER IDIOT DREAM PRANCING AROUND IN FEATHERS!
JACKASSES AND GIANT CHICKENS WITH TITS! ALL GARBAGE!!

I USED TO ENJOY MY JOB.

TELL YOUR MOTHER TO COME VISIT ME. SHE MAKES ME LAUGH. WHAT DOES SHE FIND SO FUNNY? EVERYTHING, APPARENTLY.

OLD LLOYD..
OH FANTASTIC!! ANOTHER IMBECILE CATCHING A BALL IN FRONT OF A CROWD!
HEROISM AT ITS FINEST.

WHAT'S THIS?! A MOON FELL...
!

YES--I SAW IT AND--
HRUMPH!!! TYPICAL NIGHTMARE...

HOCK
HOCK

PTOOOOO

THERE! OUTDOOR SPITTING COMPLETED!

HOORAY FOR THE RULES!
#%&!!

YOU'RE TOO YOUNG TO HAVE MET MY THIRD WIFE, HILDA.
HILDA WAS AN ARCHIVING GENIUS. SHE REARRANGED ALL YOU SEE HERE...
...NOT BY PLOT, THEME, AGE, SEX, CREED OR CLAN...

...BUT BY PURE DESIRE.

EVERY DREAM IS MADE OF DESIRE. ONE DESIRE LEADS TO ANOTHER. THE CRUELEST DESIRES INSPIRE THE KINDEST ONES, *NO KIDDING*.

YOU SEE THOSE OVER THERE?
MURDER DESIRES, RIGHT NEXT TO THE DESIRES TO TAKE IN ORPHANS.

UP THERE? THE DESIRES FOR BUTTERY PASTRIES, RIGHT ABOVE THE DESIRES TO SWIM ACROSS THE SEA.

DOWN THERE? THE DESIRES TO WIN ARGUMENTS AND GIVE AWAY FORTUNES.

SOMEDAY, IF YOU BEHAVE, I'LL SHOW YOU THE WING OF JEALOUS DESIRES. SHAMING! MAIMING! MATE THEFT! THAT'S NOT EVEN THE HALF OF IT!
IT NEVER IS...

Old Lloyd kept a lot to himself. He'd never told Eartha that he loved her like his own, or that he often saw her as a giant shade tree on a hot day.

Watching the span of her life had been like observing a stable planet that drew all surrounding debris into order. Without ever knowing it, Eartha had a way of taming chaos.

He trusted her more than anyone. Eartha was gullible, but not easily fooled about things that mattered.

He always had big plans for her, plans she never knew about.

And today he would finally put those plans into action.
NO ONE HEEDS MY ADVICE.
COUGH, COUGH..
COUGH..

I'M TOO OLD FOR THIS CRAP.
OLD LLOYD, ARE YOU ALL RIGHT?
SHHHHH!!!
COUGH, COUGH..

COUGH, COUGH! COUGH! OH, SON OF A SONOFA SON, SON, SONOFABITCH!

MY-- COUGH-- MY LAST, COUGH, SMOKE STICK...

?!
WHAT AM I GOING TO DO? I NEED THESE TO LIVE!

I GOTTA GET MORE...
SMOKE STICKS?! WHAT? HOW?

WHAT DO YOU MEAN?
COUGH.

OBSERVE, BECAUSE THIS WILL BE THE LAST TIME I'LL EVER LIGHT UP.

I PUT IT TO MY LIPS, LOVINGLY IGNITE THE END...

WATCH CLOSELY...

THERE, SEE?

IT SIPHONED ALL THE SMOKE OUT OF MY BODY.

SMOKE ACCUMULATES IN THE BODY. THIS IS A KNOWN FACT.
IT IS?
OF COURSE.

AND IT'LL AGE YOU SOMETHING AWFUL IF YOU DO NOT RELEASE IT!

WHY DO YOU THINK I LOOK SO YOUNG? IT'S THE SMOKE STICKS! I'D DIE WITHOUT THEM.

BUT THIS IS IT! THE LAST ONE, AND NOW I'M TOO DAMNED WEAK TO GO AND GET MORE...
NO..

YOU CAN'T DIE, OLD LLOYD!
TELL ME ABOUT IT! THIS PLACE WOULD FALL APART WITHOUT ME.
COUGH.

PLEASE--I'LL GET YOU MORE SMOKE STICKS! JUST TELL ME WHERE TO GO.
OH...SO... WEAK NOW...

YOU...CAN... COUGH, COUGH, GET THEM AT THE HARBOR, FROM WHAT I'VE HEARD...
COUGH, COUGH..

WHICH HARBOR, OLD LLOYD?
THE, COUGH, CITY HARBOR...

YOU'VE BEEN TO THE CITY??
OF COURSE NOT!! STRAY CRATES USED TO FLOAT HERE FROM THE CITY. I'D GATHER THEM, COUGH, COUGH...

?
BUT THAT STOPPED MONTHS AGO, ALONG WITH MY FLEETING YOUTH.
COUGH.

LLOYD, IS EVERYTHING ALL RIGHT?
GRACIE, GIVE ME YOUR HAT. I'LL EXPLAIN LATER.

COUGH
COUGH

P--PUT, COUGH, PUT THIS ON...

WHY?
YOU'RE GOING TO NEED IT FOR THE CITY...

THE CITY?? BUT--IT'S IMPOSSIBLE TO FIND!
COUGH

PEOPLE BELIEVE THAT, SURE, BUT DO THEY KNOW IT?
COUGH!

YOU'RE GOING TO LET ME DIE OVER SOME BELIEF??

Everyone in Echo Fjord knew Eartha's embrace. It was peaceful, ordered, and enveloping...

...but only Old Lloyd knew that it could lead her to places he'd never reach. She didn't know her own power. For now, such ignorance would be an advantage.

I--COUGH, NEED, COUGH, SMOKE STICKS OR...I... COUGH, COUGH, WON'T MAKE IT TO, COUGH, SUPPER.

I'LL GO.
GOOD, COUGH.

NOW TO LEAVE THE FJORD GO FIVE HUNDRED PACES BEHIND YOU, THEN TAKE A HARD RIGHT, DOWN THE PATH TO THE SCRIPTORIUM.

COUGH, DO *NOT* BOTHER THE SCRIBES THERE, EVEN IF THEY SMILE AND WAVE! GO STRAIGHT TO THE PARCHMENT CASE, PUSH IT ASIDE, AND WADE INTO THE GROTTO, GOT IT?

W--WILL I BE BACK BY SUPPER? WILL YOU STILL B--BE ALIVE?

HOW THE HELL SHOULD I KNOW?!
COUGH! PUT ME DOWN!!

YOU WANT AN OLD MAN TO DIE IN FRONT OF YOU??

GO! SMOKE STICKS! GO!!

!!
COUGH!!

WHAT WAS ALL THAT NONSENSE ABOUT SMOKE STICKS?
THAT, MY DEAR, WAS A VERY GOOD LIE.

REMEMBER THAT "FALLING MOON" DREAM I TOLD YOU ABOUT? WELL, IT FINALLY ARRIVED.
I'VE WAITED *GENERATIONS* FOR THIS DAY.

LET THE CITY BE WHAT IT WILL. ALL I CARE ABOUT IS THE PERSON WHO SENT US THAT DREAM.

Old Lloyd knew what he knew...
FOUR HUNDRED NINETY-NINE...

...FIVE HUNDRED.
...that a guileless giant...

SMOKE STICKS, SMOKE...STICKS..
...could find her way into all the right places...

...and, by her very being, solve a mystery that had haunted him for a lifetime.

I'LL SAVE YOU, OLD LLOYD..

HOW FAR AWAY IS THE CITY? IS IT BIG? HOW WILL I EVER--

--NO! HE'LL DIE WITHOUT THOSE SMOKE STICKS!

DON'T DIE, OLD LLOYD!

SCRIPTORIUM
DON'T DIE!

I'M SORRY BUT I CANNOT TALK TO YOU, EVEN IF YOU SMILE AND WAVE!

OLD LLOYD'S ORDERS!

"PARCHMENT CASE"...

"PUSH IT ASIDE"...
..."AND WADE INTO THE GROTTO."

AND... AND...

!
!

SHE'S REALLY DOING IT?
AYE.
IS THAT GRACIE'S HAT?
AYE.

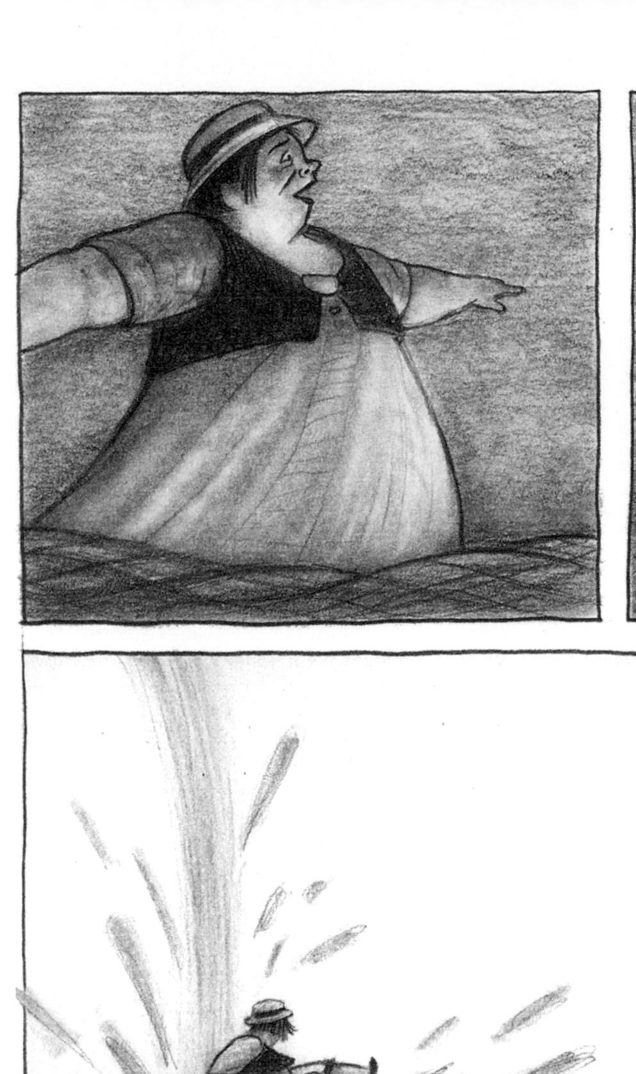

FEED

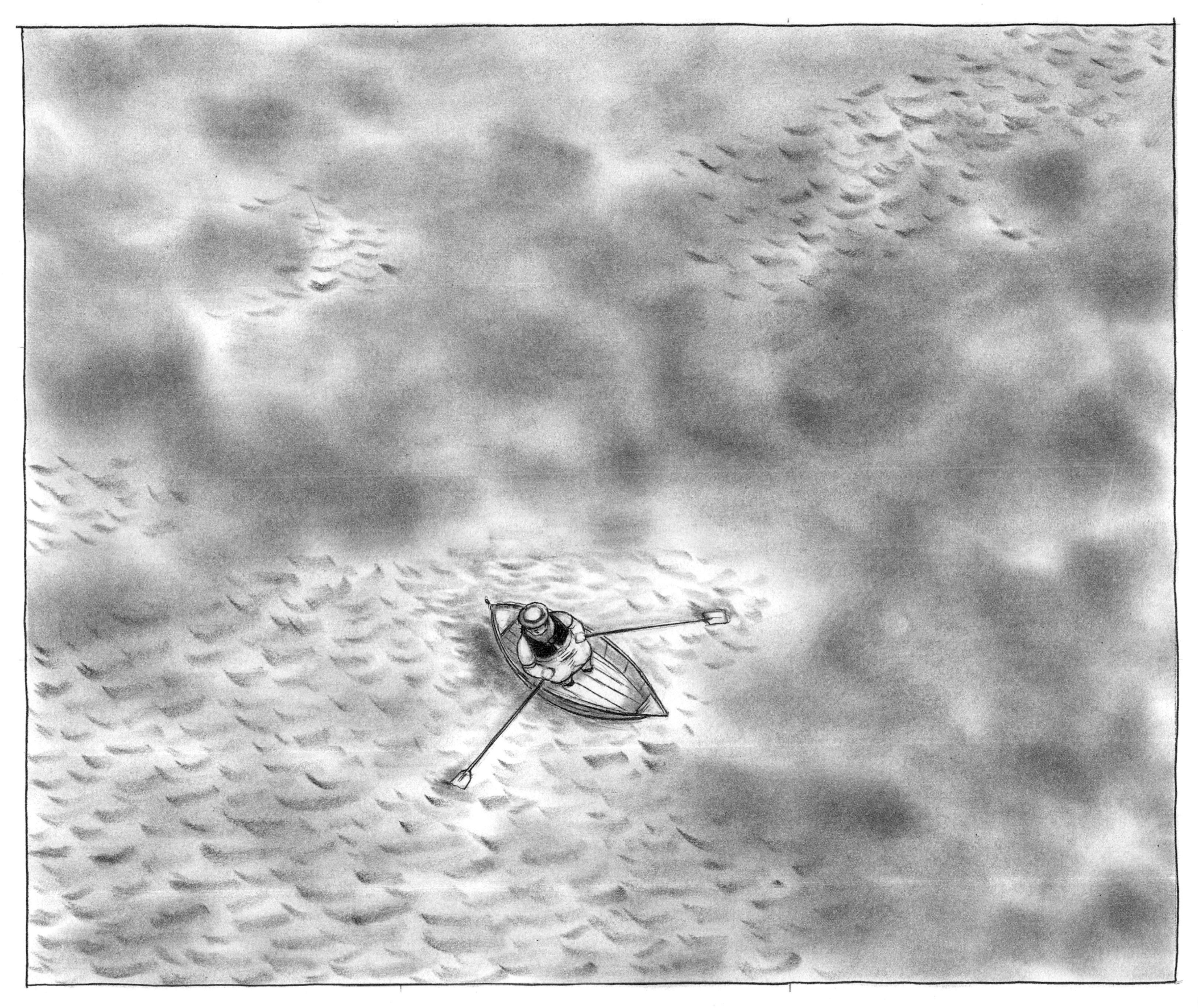

POOR OLD LLOYD...

...TOO WEAK TO TELL ME...

...WHERE TO GO.

BUT I'LL GET THERE.

MMM...
WHERE IS...
...THERE?

OH, LOOK.. THERE'S THE FJORD.

I'VE GONE FAR, THEN...

THAT'S NOT-- WHERE AM I?

...?

OLD LLOYD NEEDS HELP!

SMOKE STICKS SIPHON OUT HIS INNER SMOKE!

HE WILL DIE WITHOUT THEM!

AND...I WILL...BE HOME...
BY SUPPER!
AT LEAST THE SUN IS STILL HERE...
NO...

DON'T GO, DON'T GO!!

OH...OH!

NO...

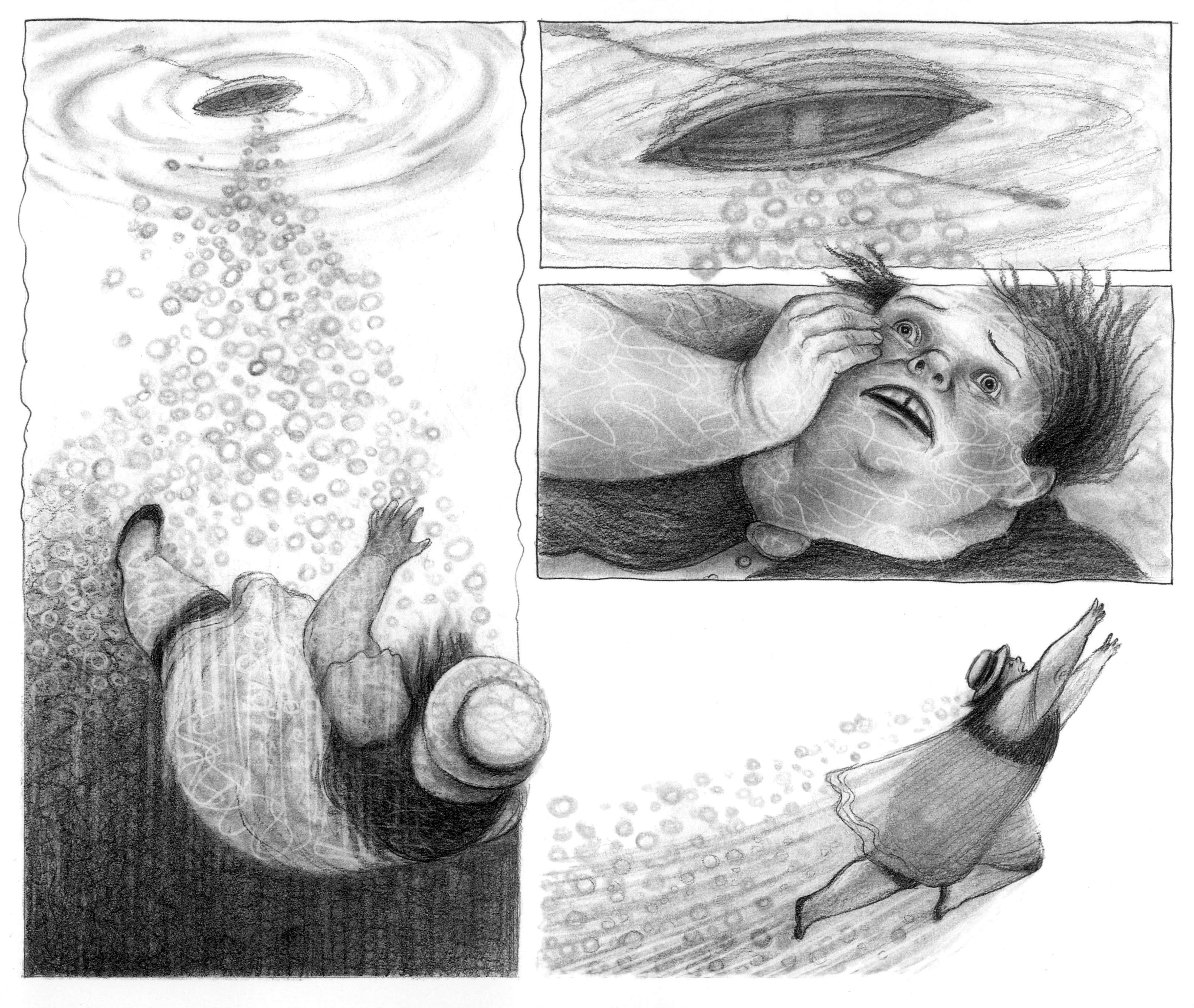

HELLO?

HELLO?

?
EVICTION

EVICTION

DIRE.
GRUESOME!
SOB.
SOB
HORRIFIC
BRUTAL..
SEXY...
SHOCKING...

LECHEROUS.
HIDEOUS.

SMOKE STICKS?

DO YOU HAVE SMOKE STICKS?

OH--SO BIG!
SO BRAVE!
?

SO... FAT!

???
DREADFUL..
GRISLY...

PLEASE-- WHERE CAN I FIND SMOKE STICKS?

PLEASE!-- MY FRIEND OLD LLOYD NEEDS THEM OR HE WILL DIE!

?
JACKASSES...

GREETINGS, SISTER!

I SALUTE YOUR COURAGE! HOW MIGHT I BE OF SERVICE?

I JUST WANT TO GET SMOKE STICKS AND LEAVE.

SOOOO... YOU WANT TO TRADE YOUR SMOKE STICKS FOR BISCUITS?

WHAT? NO... I NEED TO TRADE FOR-- *NO*, I *NEED* SMOKE STICKS.

YOUR BISCUIT, THERE. WHY AREN'T YOU EATING IT?

IT'S NOT MY BISCUIT AND I AM NOT HUNGRY.
HA, HA HA!

?
FAIR ENOUGH...

SNIFF

ARSENIC
BOMB
EVISCERATES
BABY

HEY THERE THAT'S MINE I'LL TAKE IT NOW.

IS IT TRUE?
OF COURSE IT'S TRUE.

AND OBVIOUSLY THE END OF THE WORLD IS NIGH.

BUT HEY THE **RIGHTEOUS** ARE SAFE.

WAIT...
THE END OF THE WORLD IS NIGH? HERE?

NAIL SALON
?

BISCU

EXCHANGE
BISCUIT
?!

EX

?
WHAT HAVE YOU TO TRADE?
MY WIFE'S RING.

HMM--THIS IS INSUFFICIENT TODAY.
?!

IT WAS ENOUGH YESTERDAY! PLEASE--JUST ONE BISCUIT! I HAVE TO KNOW WHAT'S GOING ON!

I WILL HELP HIM. HERE IS MY HAT.

SIR--IS THE WORLD REALLY ENDING?
SHHHH!

VERY WELL... FIVE BISCUITS.

YOU'VE TRADED GROSS MATTER FOR PURE KNOWLEDGE.

BE FREE.
NEXT!

?

B N
5 COUNT

?
CAFE
BAR
I GOT FIVE!!

WAIT!

PLEASE! SOMEONE TELL ME...

IS IT TRUE?

IS THE WORLD...

...ENDING?

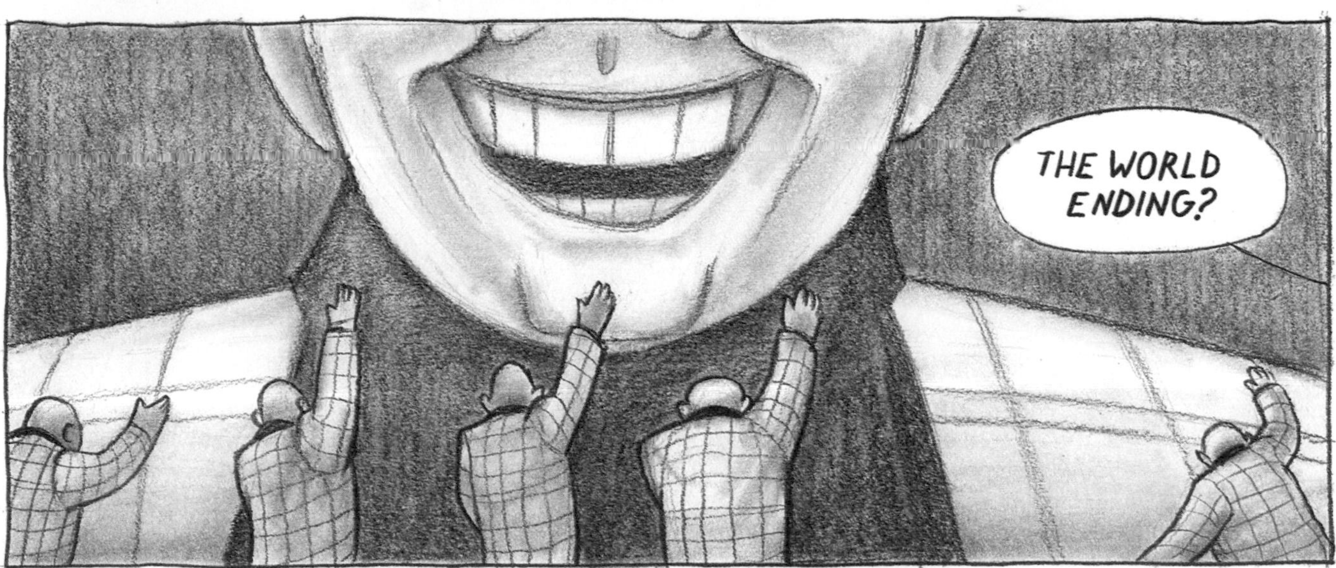
THE WORLD ENDING?

WHERE DID YOU READ THAT?!

WHERE ARE YOUR BISCUITS?
WHY ARE YOU SMILING?

SHE'S A *PRETENDER*..
YOU HAVE TO *SACRIFICE* FOR KNOWLEDGE, YOU KNOW.

JUST ANOTHER CHUBBY BUMPKIN.
?

EARN YOUR OWN BISCUITS...
... OR GET OUT!!

???

?

"BISCUIT NEWS"?
BN
BISCUIT NEWS
"The World in a Bite!"
HORRIBLE!
SOB.
BAR
CAFÉ
"The World in a Bite"

I AM FAT, FAT, FAT!

YES, HOW VERY FAT YOU ARE!
PLEASE, TO THE CAFE..
SORRY, LADIES. WITH THOSE FIGURES YOU'LL HAVE TO EAT OUTSIDE.

MY STARS.
ARE YOU CERTAIN?
MA'AM, IF IT ISN'T ON A BISCUIT...
...IT ISN'T SO.
?

LOOK AT THEM.
ANIMALS.
!
INFERIOR.

"The World in a Bite
?
OH NO...

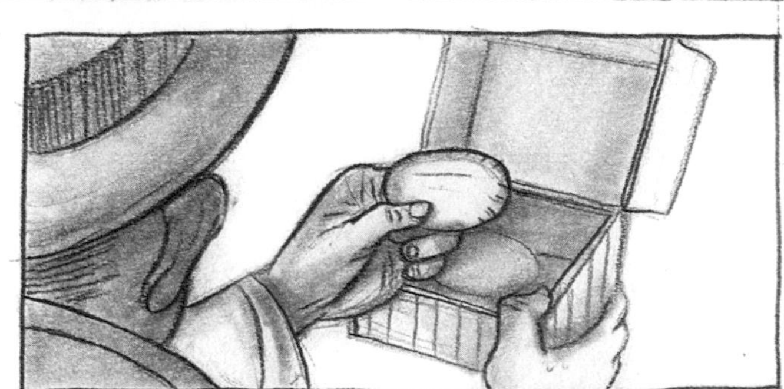

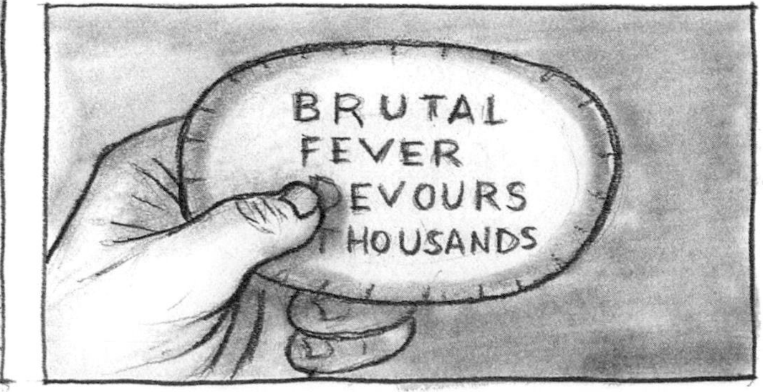
BRUTAL
FEVER
DEVOURS
THOUSANDS

OH NO,
OH NO!!!

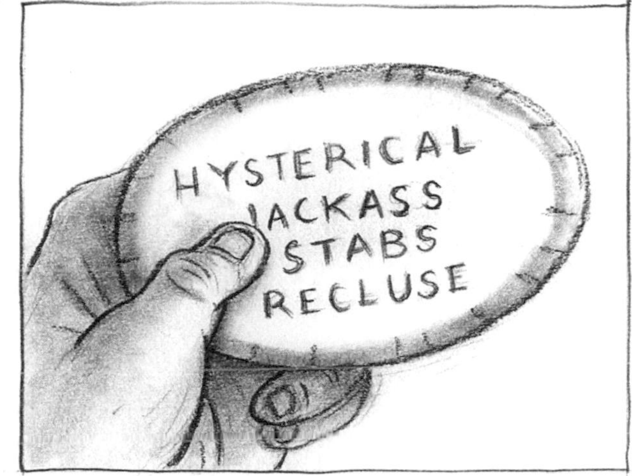
HYSTERICAL
JACKASS
STABS
RECLUSE

OH MY
STARS!

HEY..

THIS BISCUIT IS MINE. THIS KNOWLEDGE IS FOR ME!
IT IS ALL HORRIBLE AND I AM IN PAIN!

BUT--IS THAT A REAL THING?
OF COURSE IT'S A REAL THING!

?
BUT--
GO AWAY!
?

PSSSST...

PRETEND YOU'VE FOUND ME AFTER A LONG SEARCH.

WHY?

BECAUSE YOU WANT TO LIVE.

NICE CAT!
WILL YOU BE TRADING IT TODAY?
SAY "YES" AND SMILE.
YES AND SMILE!

PRRRRRR

WHAT WERE YOU DOING OUT THERE?
I... DON'T KNOW.

UNLESS YOU'VE GOT BISCUITS STAY OUTA THERE, UNDERSTAND?

THOSE THINGS THEY'RE READING--ON THE BISCUITS--ARE THEY TRUE?
WHO WANTS TO KNOW?

ARE YOU DIM OR NAIVE? PUT ME DOWN! I'M GETTING RESTLESS.

WHAT IS IT ABOUT YOU? I FEEL STRANGE..

EVERYONE LOOKED PAINED BY WHAT THEY READ, BUT THEY DIDN'T DO ANYTHING TO FEEL BETTER.
THEY *ATE*, DIDN'T THEY?
BUT THEY ATE THE THINGS THAT UPSET THEM.
WHY DO YOU CARE?

AND STAY AWAY FROM THE GUYS IN PLAID JACKETS!
WHY?

BECAUSE THEY'RE THE **BOUNCERS**! DANGEROUS.

I DON'T WANT ANY GAMES, UNDERSTAND? WHERE ARE YOU FROM? THE CONTINENT?
NO.

YOU SMELL...HUMBLE. LIGHT BENDS AT YOUR EDGES. ARE YOU SOME KIND OF SPY?
NO. I JUST NEED SMOKE STICKS.

SMOKE STICKS? NOW I'VE HEARD EVERYTHING! YOU MAKE NO SENSE AT ALL, AND YET I FEEL NOTHING BUT SENSE AROUND YOU.

I'LL EXPLAIN.
FOLLOW ME UP.

SEE THAT? IT'S THE MOST POWERFUL ANTENNA IN THE WORLD.
NEWS

IT GETS THE NEWS FROM EVERYWHERE AT EVERY MOMENT.

THE NEWS GETS PRINTED ONTO BISCUITS. PEOPLE READ THEM AND DEVOUR THEM.

THEY NEVER FEEL QUITE FULL, BUT THEY'RE CERTAIN THEY KNOW EVERYTHING THERE IS TO KNOW.
THEY SEEM SO BUSY.

OF COURSE THEY'RE BUSY! THEY'RE IN GREAT PAIN.
PAIN?

WHEN YOU KNOW TOO MUCH OF THE WORLD YOU FEEL DESPAIR, RIGHT?

WHY IS THE NEWS PRINTED ON BISCUITS?

IF KNOWLEDGE BRINGS YOU AGONY THEN YOU'RE GOING TO NEED A LITTLE COMFORT...

NEWS AND PASTRY-- PROBLEM AND SOLUTION IN ONE BUTTERY BITE!

EVERYONE GETS THEIR OWN UNIQUE TREATS. THEY PAY HANDSOMELY, YOU KNOW.

ARE YOU JOKING?
HA!--I *WISH*. YOU SEE THAT LADY DOWN THERE? WITH THE BIG HAIR?

TWENTY!
I GOT *TWENTY!*

SHE JUST TRADED HER FOX TERRIER FOR A MERE TWENTY BISCUITS. I MET GUS-- YES, HE HAD A SPEECH IMPEDIMENT, BUT HE WAS A LOYAL WATCHDOG.

TWENTY BISCUITS!

THAT'S HOW MUCH I CARE-- *TWENTY!*

SHE *TRADED HIM!* ALONG WITH MONEY, FAMILY HEIRLOOMS, STOCKS, PROPERTY-- ALL TO GET A LITTLE BAD NEWS ON PASTRY.

SHE DOESN'T CARE THAT YESTERDAY THE BOUNCERS INFLATED BISCUIT VALUES. SHE DOESN'T MIND THAT THEY AIM TO FLEECE HER OF EVERY POSSESSION...
I GOT TWENTY!
WORLD PAIN CAFE

GASP!
SHE JUST WANTS TO KNOW WHAT SHE KNOWS, AND LET EVERYONE KNOW SHE KNOWS IT.

IS THIS YOUR HOME?
NO. IT WAS HERS. SHE TRADED IT.

AND THIS IS MY TRIBUTE TO GUS.

SO MUCH FOR LOYALTY.

LAST WEEK PEOPLE TRADED SO MANY SHOES FOR BISCUITS THAT SHOE VALUES PLUMMETED. THREE PAIR GOT YOU ONE BISCUIT, WHILE A SINGLE TOOTHBRUSH GOT YOU FIVE.

CAFE
SCUFFLES BROKE OUT AND THE BOUNCERS SUPPRESSED THEM, WITH THEIR USUAL PLEASURE.
PLEASURE?
BAR
PEDICU
BAR

BEING CHASTE MAKES 'EM BETTER FIGHTERS.
THEY'RE-- CELIBATE?
DON'T ASK..

WELL, WELL-- SHE'S MADE IT TO THE FRONT OF THE LINE! THIS IS HER FIRST VISIT TO A WORLD PAIN CAFE.
?
I...HOLD SUCH... HORRIBLE NEWS!!
COME IN, FAT SISTER!

THERE SHE'LL SIT ALL MORNING, EATING AND PUBLICLY WAILING OVER ALL HER BAD NEWS.

THE EATING AND WAILING GET VERY COMPETITIVE.
SOB!
SOB!
SOB.

HOW'D YOU GET SO HUSKY? DO YOU EAT A LOT OF EVERYTHING?
NO. I'VE BEEN LARGE A LONG TIME.

LUCKY YOU! YOUR SIZE IS THE REASON THE BOUNCERS ARE LEAVING YOU ALONE.

THEY ASSUME YOU'RE UPPER CLASS. AROUND HERE GIRTH EQUALS STATUS.

WHY?

THE FATTER YOU ARE, THE MORE BISCUIT NEWS YOU'VE EATEN! YOUR FAT IS A BADGE! IT SHOWS EVERYONE JUST HOW MUCH YOU'VE SACRIFICED TO KNOW THE WORLD!

OH, LOOK! HERE COMES ANOTHER MARTYR...

WORLD PAIN CAFE
KNOWLEDGE LOUNGE
SOB, SOB! I'VE CONSUMED SEVEN HUNDRED TODAY AND MY PAIN IS HUGE.
BROTHER, I SALUTE YOUR COURAGE! PLEASE FIND YOUR WAY TO THE V.I.P. LOUNGE.
MASSAGE

WHO IS THE SMILING MAN ON THE SIGN?
THAT'S MR. BISCUIT. HE'S THE FACE OF BISCUIT NEWS. HE DIED LAST WEEK. ONLY THE BOUNCERS KNOW HE'S GONE. FOR NOW, AT LEAST...
...OUT TO GET US!
NOT AGAIN!
"The World in a Bite"
SOB!
IT'S HOPELESS!

THEY DRESS LIKE HIM, SMILE LIKE HIM, PRAISE HIS GENIUS, AND MAKE SURE THERE'S ALWAYS A STEADY BISCUIT SUPPLY.

BISCUITS ON EVERY MIND, BISCUITS IN EVERY GUT...
SOB!
SOB!
PEOPLE ARE TERRIFIED AND THEY DON'T KNOW WHY..

NOBODY SLEEPS! AFRAID THEY'LL MISS OUT! THEY DON'T TRAVEL OUTSIDE THE CITY, AFRAID OF MISSING THEIR NEWS FROM OUTSIDE THE CITY! THEY WANT TO BE HERE, YET THEY'D RATHER BE ANYWHERE BUT HERE!

SOB
AND THEY SAY MY SPECIES IS DIM!

YOU ALL RIGHT?

KNOWING THE WORLD THROUGH LITTLE BISCUITS-- IS THIS REAL?
OH, IT'S REAL, ALL RIGHT...

LATELY EVEN DREAMING IS NO MATCH FOR BAD NEWS! YOU CAN THANK PRIMUS FOR THAT

SISTER!
SPEAK OF THE DEVIL...

WAIT! WHERE ARE YOU GOING?

SISTER!!

HELLO THERE!

!!
!!!
OH NO...
OH NO WHAT?
!!!!!

Eartha could not believe her eyes: only hours ago she and Maybelle had watched this man's dream cavort with fowl delights...
...and now...

...Her voyage had forced an uneasy reunion.

Suddenly Eartha knew both the dreamer and his innermost dream -- a betrayal of the Fjord's solemn oath.
?

Eartha panicked. What would Maybelle do? What would she say?

Eartha felt entirely alone.
SISTER, WHAT IS THE MATTER?
NOTHING.

WHY ARE YOU NOT EATING?
I AM NOT...HUNGRY.
SWEET SISTER, I AM CONFUSED AND CONCERNED! SHALL I LOOK AFTER YOUR BISCUIT NEEDS PERSONALLY?

I...I AM LOOKING ...FOR...MY CAT...
HA, HA! YOU'RE CHARMING.

YOUR **GIRTH** AROUSES ME, BUT *DO NOT FEAR!* I AM IN FULL CONTROL OF MY IMPULSES.

ARE YOU WALKING AWAY FROM ME? THAT IS MOST UNWISE.

DO YOU NOT KNOW WHO I AM?

THEY CALL ME PRIMUS FOR A REASON! I AM LEADER OF ALL BOUNCERS.

APPOINTED BY MR. BISCUIT HIMSELF, I AM INDISPUTABLY PURE.

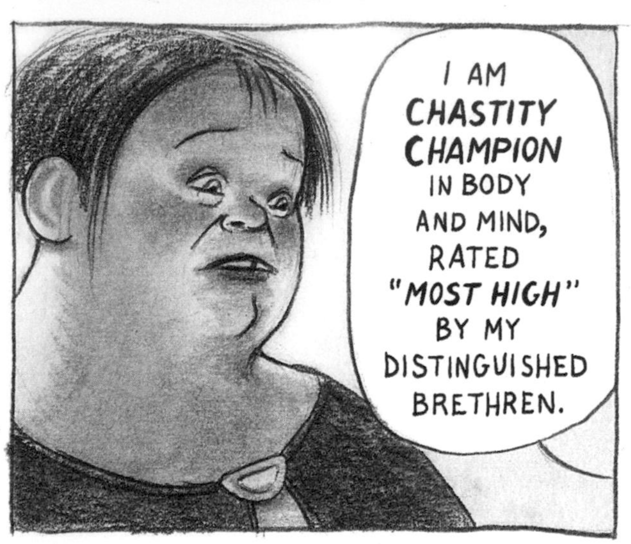
I AM CHASTITY CHAMPION IN BODY AND MIND, RATED "MOST HIGH" BY MY DISTINGUISHED BRETHREN.

BODILY IMPULSES WREACK HAVOC ON CIVIC LIFE. MAY I, SISTER? WHY, THANK YOU...

?
THAT'S IT! DO NOT BE AFRAID! WHAT A MODEL CITIZEN YOU ARE! I AM READING YOUR IMPULSE LEVEL, WHICH IS CONVEYED, OF COURSE, THROUGH THE BREASTS...

YOUR--OH--IMPULSE, OH--LEVEL IS--OH--ADMIRABLY LOW...

YOU ARE--OH--IN CONTROL OF YOUR IMPULSES...

I SALUTE YOU.
YOU MAY GO NOW.
QUICKLY!

RESIST, PRIMUS...

THINK OF CHICKENS..

THINK OF CHICKENS!
AGH..
AAAGH.

AAAGGHGGH!!

!!

OH NO.

PRIMUS, SIR!

WHAT IS IT, BROTHERS?
REQUESTING LEAVE FROM ANTENNA DUTIES, SIR!
GRANTED. SHIFT OVER.

AND BROTHERS, I ALERT YOU TO A BUXOM SHE-BUMPKIN ROAMING OUR STREETS. SHE IS LARGE, RETICENT, AND SUSPICIOUSLY SATED. LOCATE HER, MONITOR HER EVERY MOVEMENT, AND REPORT TO ME.
YESSIR!!

At such points he could feel his desire leave him, soaring to some faraway place...

...as if he'd launched a part of himself through the city walls and out to another world.

Meantime he had amassed great wealth simply by providing order to a needlessly desperate people.

Primus created the **Brotherhood of Bouncers**, the City's only sales team and morality force.

With a few exceptions, the Bouncers were grateful to Primus, considering him a visionary, the confidant and spiritual advisor to their Great Leader.
STEADY ON, LADS!

RECITE!
It was Primus who had fashioned their creed...
...out of whispers he'd overheard from Mr. Biscuit himself.

I AM NOTHING BUT A WOEFUL TANGLE OF NERVES!
AND I WILL NEVER, EVER TOUCH HER AGAIN!
JUST STRAY SIGNALS, IMPULSES AND EMPTY PATTERNS...
...AND I WILL NEVER, EVER TOUCH HER AGAIN!
I AM THE CHAOS THAT TRICKS ITSELF INTO ORDER!

MEANING IS A PHANTOM...

...CONNECTION IS AN ILLUSION...

...ACQUISITION IS JUSTICE...
...AND MATTER IS ALL THAT MATTERS!

SMILE, FELLAS! TODAY WE CHANGE THE WORLD!
...Primus urged his troops, even after receiving the fateful news.

Exactly one week ago he learned of Mr. Biscuit's death. He told a trusted deputy, who informed the other Bouncers.

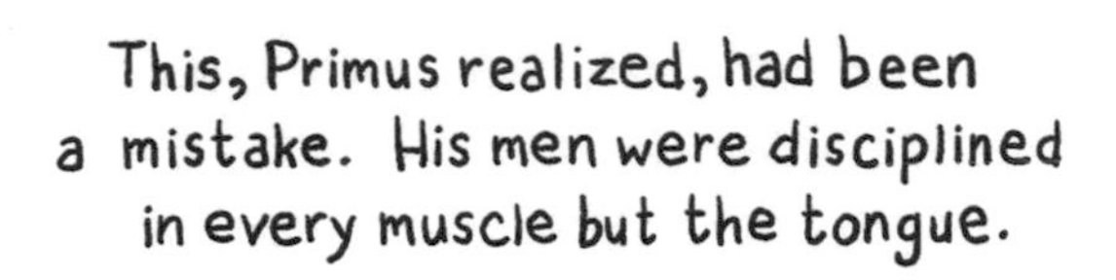
This, Primus realized, had been a mistake. His men were disciplined in every muscle but the tongue.

DISMISSED!
YESSIR!

It was only a matter of time before some would invent stories against him, now that he no longer had the ear of their idol.
A coup seemed inevitable, but he was certain he could weather it.

ANIMALS...
Still, he grew to hate his men and their in-fighting. Their squabbles rattled the Biscuit market, stirring worries over the Biscuit supply. They had learned his game: incite panic...

...and watch the very profitable reaction.
"ACQUISITION...
...IS JUSTICE"

Primus knew his destiny: to own every brick in the City, and exhaust its rapt populace into complete surrender.
YOU-- COME HERE.
?

He had studied well their expressions and possessions, cobbling together a system that put their inner turmoil under his control...
QUIET! KEEP STILL..

To own everything was to know everything...
CAREFUL, SISTER...
YOU ARE PRONE TO WEAKNESS...

MANAGE YOUR IMPULSES!

...and to know everything was Order.

WORLD PAIN CAFE
...but Order had shunned him today.

Primus knew that something from Beyond had nudged him, that a stranger had stormed the city and rearranged his insides.
!!?

He hated the She-Bumpkin...
THINK OF CHICKENS...
THINK OF CHICKENS!
...and he had to find her.

AND HERE ARE THE KEYS TO MY MOTHER'S HOME. ENJOY IT IN GOOD HEALTH!
AND HERE ARE YOUR UP-TO-THE-MINUTE BISCUITS, ALL ONE THOUSAND OF THEM. BROTHER, WE SALUTE YOUR COURAGE!
DO I LOOK FAT?
YOU CERTAINLY DO!
EVICTION
Z Z Z
1,000 COUNT

?

WAKE UP, SISTER!
Z Z Z

YOU DON'T WANT TO MISS OUT!

PLEASE--I'M SO TIRED...
BUT THERE'S SO MUCH TO EAT! SO MUCH TO KNOW!

I'LL GIVE YOU TWENTY BISCUITS FOR THE SUITCASE!
YOU HEARD THE MAN, MAMA!

?
PFFFT

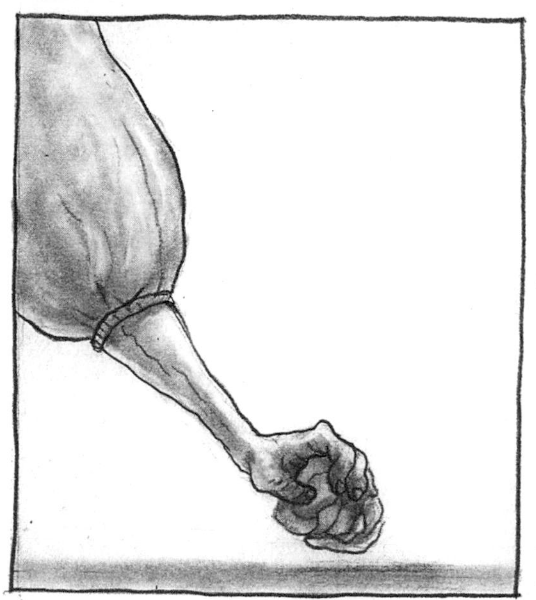

I CAN'T LEAVE HERE YET...

...NOT IF THOSE BOUNCERS ARE KEEPING PEOPLE FROM DREAMING!

I HAVE TO HELP.

BUT HOW?

I CAN'T BELIEVE MR. BISCUIT'S DEAD.

YOU THINK WE'LL KEEP THE CHASTITY RULE?
OF COURSE. IT'S IN THE CREED.

THE CREED THAT PRIMUS GAVE US.
YEAH... GOOD OL' "PRIMUS"...

YES, AND PRIMUS GAVE US AN ORDER TO FIND THE LARGE SHE-BUMPKIN.
YESSIR--I MEANT NO DISRESPECT...

BROTHER, LOOK! IS THAT HER?

VOYEUR JACKASS DEFILES SOFA

THAT POOR SOFA!

Greatest Pain
LIQUOR HOUSE
THIS IS HORRIBLE, SIMPLY TOO HORRIBEE!
WELCOME, SISTERS.

MY PAIN IS GREAT.

?!
MY PAIN IS GREAT!

BRUTAL!
SOB
THOUSANDS DEAD!
JACKASSES!
SOB!
SOB...
ZZZ
SOB!
I KNEW IT.
SOB.
PERVERTS!

IT'S JUST TOO MUCH...

TOO MUCH!!

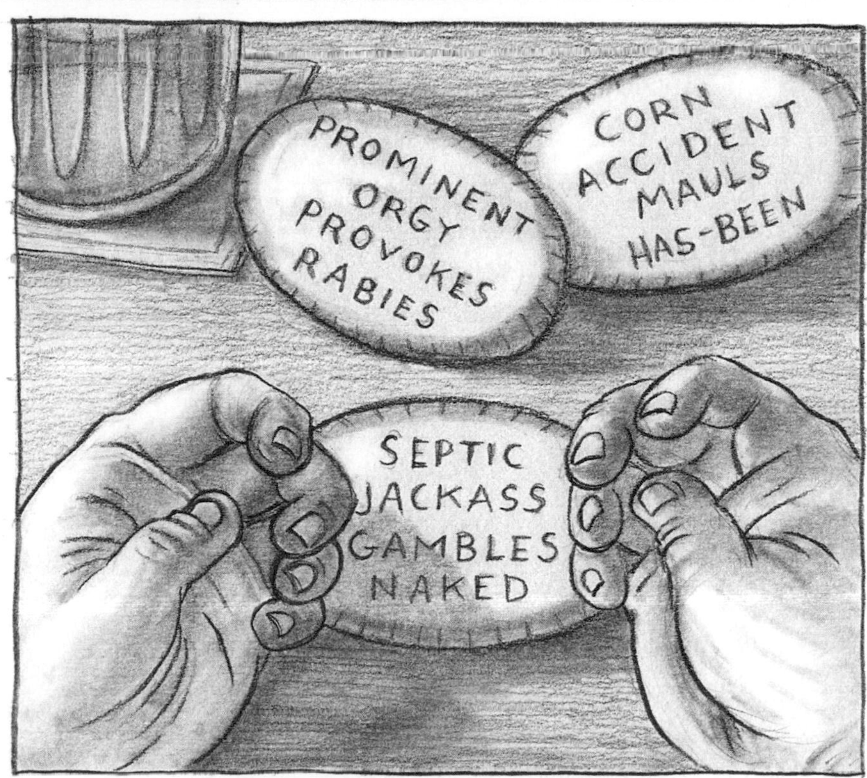
PROMINENT ORGY PROVOKES RABIES
CORN ACCIDENT MAULS HAS-BEEN
SEPTIC JACKASS GAMBLES NAKED

IT'S A RAVAGED WORLD...

ZZzzz
FRENZIED JACKASS TARGETS CASABA
SEXY JACKASS INFECTS FONDUE

ZZZZ

ZZZ

ZZZ

WHAT DID I MISS?
YOU NEED TO SLEEP, TO DREAM! THAT WILL MAKE YOU FEEL BETTER.

HOW CAN I SLEEP?! THE JACKASSES ARE TAKING OVER...

THE WORLD'S GOING TO HELL AND WE ARE DAMNED LUCKY TO BE THE FIRST TO KNOW!

WE'RE DAMNED LUCKY.. zzz... ...SAFE.. zzz.. ..FREE...
THAT'S IT: DREAM...

ZZZ
I'LL GET THIS WHOLE CITY TO DREAM AGAIN.

KEEP YOUR EYES PEELED, BROTHER...
YESSIR!
SOB!
SOB

NOT HER..
SOB!
SOB!
SOB!
SOB.

STOP, BROTHER, AND SALUTE MR. BISCUIT.

REMEMBER BROTHER PRIMUS'S ORDERS.

ZZZ
YOU DON'T UNDERSTAND.. I USED TO BE ADDICTED TO FOREIGN THINGS...

...THINGS FROM EVERYWHERE BUT HERE! THE BISCUITS CURED ME. THEY GAVE ME A REASON TO LIVE.

I AM DOING MY PART.

ISN'T THAT--
OH YES.

"LARGE AND RETICENT."

LET'S BRING HER IN!
PATIENCE, BROTHER...

MY PAIN IS GREATEST!
AND I WIIL PROCLAIM IT!!

I WILL SAY MY PIECE!!
MY BISCUIT IS IMPORTANT!!!
EASY, FELLA...

Z Z Z
AND I WANT TO TELL THE WORLD!

YOU'RE A BRAVE MAN...
SOB
SOB
...READING ABOUT THE STRUGGLES OF OTHERS...

I... KNOW THINGS!
OF COURSE, AND YOU'VE SACFRIFICED ALL YOU HAVE...

??
...AND WE ARE GRATEFUL TO OCCUPY YOUR FORMER HOME.

DID YOU KNOW THAT I'M SLEEPING IN YOUR DEAR MOTHER'S OLD ROOM?

MY, MY, HOW SHE MUST'VE LOVED THOSE LACE CURTAINS...

BLESS YOU, BROTHER! I AM HONORED.

PROTECT US, BROTHERS! THE JACKASSES-- THE JACKASSES!!

ZZZ

THAT'S IT-- SLEEP!
ZZZZ
ZZZ

I WILL PROTECT YOU...
ZZZ
ZZZ

JUST SEND US YOUR DREAMS.
ZZZ
ZZZZZ

WE WILL CARE...
...FOR ALL THE DREAMS...

...YOU CANNOT KEEP...

ZZZ
ZZZ

??
WHERE I LIVE YOUR DREAMS VISIT FREELY.
ZZ

WHY IS SHE HANDLING THEM?

THAT'S *OUR* JOB!
EASY..

PRIMUS SAID TO FOLLOW HER...

...FIND OUT WHO SHE'S WORKING FOR...

YOUR DREAMS STAY WITH US UNTIL THEY'RE DONE.
ZZZZ

SNIFF, SNIFF--- **SMOKE STICKS!**

ZZZ
ZZZZ
JACKASS THIS, JACKASS THAT-- I'LL TELL YOU WHO'S THE JACKASS...

...MY OWN SON! HE TRADED MY APARTMENT FOR A HUNDRED BISCUITS! SAID WE HAD TO "STAY INFORMED TO BE SAFE."

I ALMOST GOT EATEN BY RATS LAST NIGHT. HOW SAFE IS THAT?!

"NEWS."
MY DAUGHTER AND HER FARAWAY DANGERS--HA! THE REAL DANGER'S RIGHT HERE...
...IN PLAID JACKETS!

THEY CLOSED THE MUSEUM AND PUT IN A NAIL SALON. THE WHOLE DAMNED CITY'S FALLING APART...
...AND NOBODY EVEN SEES IT, WALKING AROUND LIKE GHOSTS.

"IF IT ISN'T ON A BISCUIT"...
..."IT ISN'T SO!" GARBAGE!

?
?

CHUBBY LADY, SHOULDN'T YOU BE IN SOME POSH CAFE?

SOB.
LOOK AT HER GLOAT...
FAKE TEARS!

SOB
GOT SOME BAD NEWS, DID YA'?
WONDER WHAT SHE TRADED FOR IT, THE COW...

SOB
HOLD ON...
THOSE TEARS ARE REAL!

OH DEAR! YOU'RE NOT A COW.
SIT DOWN, SWEETHEART..

HOW COULD THEY TAKE YOUR HOMES AWAY?
SOB

WHERE YOU FROM, DEAR?
SOMEWHERE ELSE...
AN IMMIGRANT... WELL, LEAVE HERE WHILE YOU CAN...

WHAT IS HAPPENING?
NOTHING! THAT'S THE PROBLEM...

THEN A WEEK AGO --NO WARNING!-- BISCUIT VALUES WENT THROUGH THE ROOF...
EVERYONE'S MORE HOOKED THAN EVER.

IT'S ALL A GAME AND WE'RE STUCK IN IT.
THE BOUNCERS TAKE EVERYTHING.

AND FOR WHAT?

SO THAT FOOLS CAN OWN THE BRAGGING RIGHTS TO BAD NEWS, PANTOMIMING CONCERN, OR CYNICISM, OR WORLDLINESS, ALL FOR THINGS THEY'LL NEVER TOUCH OR TASTE...

GIVE US BACK OUR HOMES!
?!

TSK, TSK... YOUR HOMES WERE FAIRLY TRADED...

YOU'VE RUINED THIS CITY!

YOU ARE MISTAKEN! WE ONLY SEEK TO COMFORT THOSE IN THEIR TIME OF NEED.

BY MAKING THEM CRAZY WITH THOSE POINTLESS BISCUITS?

POINTLESS?! TO KNOW EVERYTHING AS IT HAPPENS IS A MORAL DUTY, SIR...
AND WHAT'S YOUR DUTY? KILLING? TAKING EVERYTHING WE HAVE?

WE ARE TAKING US ALL BACK TO A PURER TIME, BEFORE STRIFE AND CHAOS.

A PROFITABLE CHAOS! THAT'S WHERE YOU'RE TAKING US!
??

I WANT MY BED BACK, AND MY COFFEE POT, AND MY WIFE'S LETTERS, AND MY TOOLS.

WE'VE MADE USE OF YOUR BED, READ THOSE SWEET LETTERS, MELTED THE TOOLS, AND PISSED IN THE COFFEE POT.

WHAT? YOU CAN'T DO THAT! SHE'S DEAD! HER LETTERS... THOSE WERE FOR ME!
!!

IS THAT... HER... EARRING?

WHY, YES. THREE BISCUITS. A FAIR TRADE, WOULDN'T YOU SAY?

SHHHH.
GIVE IT BACK! I AM NOT AFRAID OF YOU!!

YOU'RE...YOU'RE CRUSHING MY HAND.

?!

ZZZZ
?

ZZZ
???

Primus cherished his talent for cruelty. It was meant to carry him to this day, one he had long planned for...

...to stage one or two public executions and cement his hold on power.

He hadn't planned on a sudden and overwhelming embrace.
Eartha's touch obliterated his schemes, making him feel like a tiny body...

...drawn into a great orbit.

The She-Bumpkin was all surprises, a door onto other worlds. He yearned to be in countless elsewheres, with her...
...but he would resist.

WHY DO YOU KEEP THEM FROM DREAMING?
OH, SISTER...

YOU ARE **NOT** IN CONTROL OF YOUR IMPULSES.

WHO ARE YOU?
I AM **NOT** YOUR SISTER.

DO YOU THINK YOU CAN STOP **ME**? I'LL SNUFF YOU OUT.

I'VE TORN A HOLE IN THE SKY AND LOOKED BACK TO THE BEGINNING... YOU'LL ***NEVER*** FATHOM MY POWER.
THEY CAN'T MAKE THE WORLD IF THEY CAN'T DREAM.

YOU LET ***ME*** HANDLE HOW THE WORLD IS MADE!

YOU FEED THEM BUT KEEP THEIR SPIRITS STARVED...
ENOUGH!

I OWN EVERY BRICK IN THIS CITY, BECAUSE ANIMALS LIKE YOU CAN'T CONTROL THEMSELVES...

...AND WHATEVER YOU THINK YOU'RE DOING TO ME, YOU WILL **FAIL**.

I AM NOT ONE OF YOUR BIG-TITTED *CHICKENS*...
?!

WHO ARE YOU? WHY ARE YOU HERE??

HOW DO YOU GET YOUR INFORMATION?

YOU ARE A **BEAST**. I AM **REPULSED** AT THE **SIGHT** OF YOU...

I'VE SWEPT UP SHADOWS THAT WEIGH MORE THAN YOU.

WHAT DO YOU KNOW ABOUT *ANYTHING*?

?!
ABOUT HARDSHIP? ABOUT BEING *NOTHING*? ABOUT A HIGHER ORDER?!

YOU SAY THOSE WORDS WITH NO FEELING...
SHUT UP!!

BROTHERS! GET HER OUT OF HERE!

DO WE KILL HER, PRIMUS?

NO, NO, NO, NOT YET.
PUT HER TO WORK IN THE BAKERY.
YESSIR!

JUST ANOTHER FILTHY BISCUIT ADDICT WANTING SOMETHING FOR NOTHING...

WHY CAN'T WE TAKE HER TO THE BRIDGE?
PRIMUS SAID THE BAKERY!
NICE IMPULSES, SISTER!

LEAVE HER ALONE!

STAY PURE, BROTHER.
LET SOMEONE ELSE USE HER.

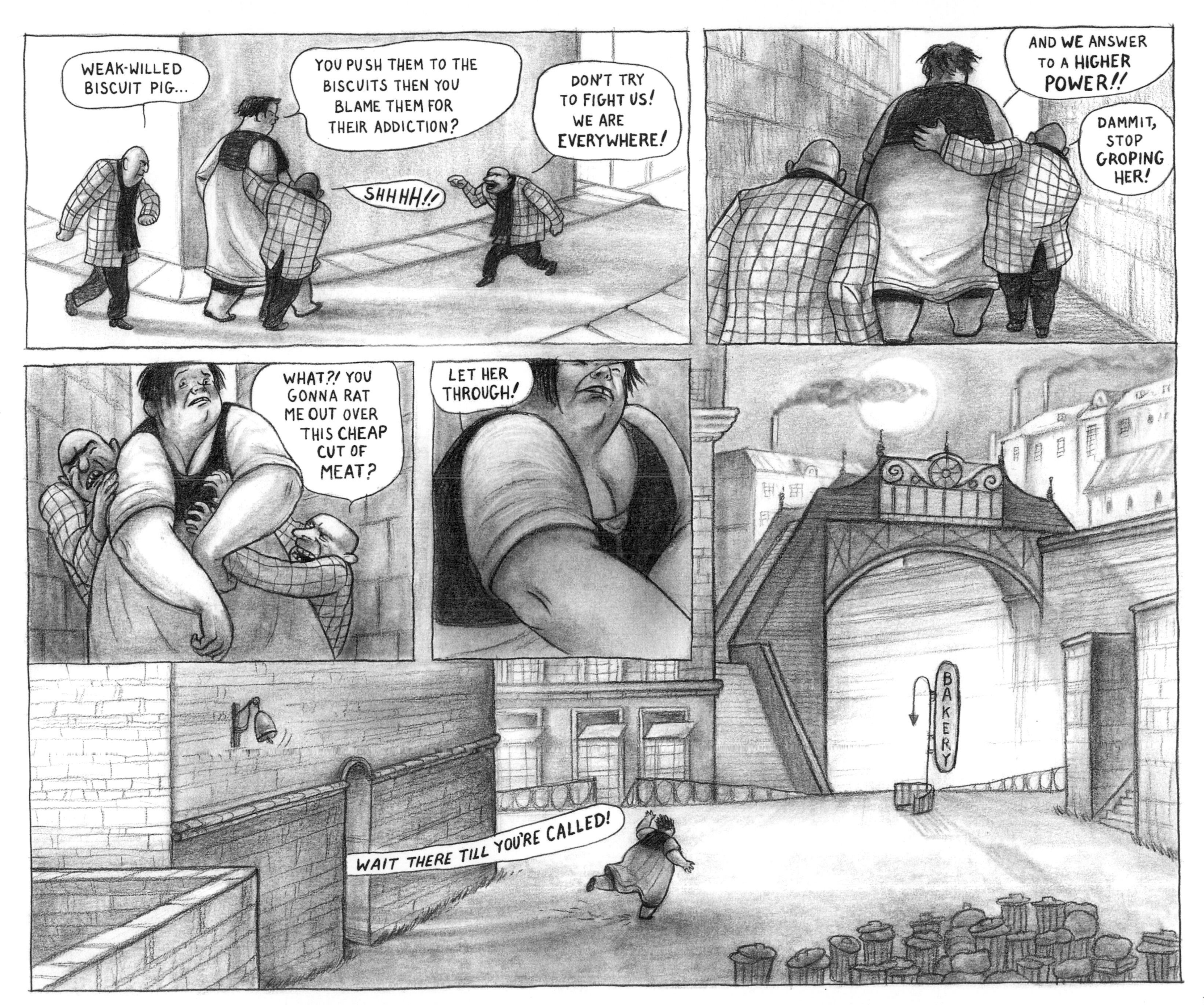
WEAK-WILLED BISCUIT PIG...
YOU PUSH THEM TO THE BISCUITS THEN YOU BLAME THEM FOR THEIR ADDICTION?
DON'T TRY TO FIGHT US! WE ARE EVERYWHERE!
SHHHH!!
AND WE ANSWER TO A HIGHER POWER!!
DAMMIT, STOP GROPING HER!
WHAT?! YOU GONNA RAT ME OUT OVER THIS CHEAP CUT OF MEAT?
LET HER THROUGH!
BAKERY
WAIT THERE TILL YOU'RE CALLED!

THE FJORD SUN IS BETTER. THIS SUN IS TOO BRIGHT AND ROUND.
... AND COLD.

LET THEM SORT THEMSELVES OUT! I'LL GET THE SMOKE STICKS AND GO BACK TO OLD LLOYD.

I DON'T CARE IF THEY NEVER DREAM AGAIN! WE DON'T NEED THEIR THOUGHTS...

"FINDING JOY IN WHAT WE CAN'T EXPLAIN."
I CAN'T FIND JOY HERE, MAYBELLE...
OH... I MISS YOU.
I MISS EVERYONE..

AHEM.

SORRY I HAD TO LEAVE YOU. BOUNCERS ENJOY KICKING CATS...

MAY I?
OF COURSE.

YOU KNOW, PRRRRRRRR IT CAN BE A BURDEN, TO KNOW TOO MUCH...

I'VE BEEN WATCHING PRIMUS. HE'S HAD EVERYTHING HANDED TO HIM, BUT HE'S NEVER SATISFIED.
PRRRRRR...

HE PLEASURES HIMSELF ON A STRICT HOURLY SCHEDULE. I DON'T JUDGE...
PRRRR

...BUT THEN THERE'S HIS AMBITION. I'VE HEARD HIM MAKING PLANS TO KILL EVERY THREAT.

NOW THAT MR. BISCUIT'S DEAD, *EVERYONE* IS A THREAT.
I'M... *SCARED.*

YES.
HE LOOKS AT THE WORLD WITH SOUR EYES. HE THINKS HE SHOULD LIVE FOREVER. DO YOU KNOW WHAT I MEAN?

I THOUGHT YOU WOULD UNDERSTAND. YOU'RE LIKE A CAT, AREN'T YOU? ALWAYS THINKING. I MUST ADMIT I LIKED YOU RIGHT AWAY.

SAY, DO YOU THINK THAT HUMAN CRUELTY IS A NECESSARY PART OF NATURE? I CAN'T HELP BUT WONDER, ESPECIALLY ON A DAY WHEN A CAT'S VALUE HAS DROPPED TO ONE BISCUIT...

SOMETIMES I IMAGINE ALL OF THIS IS JUST A BAD DREAM...

SOB
SOB
SOB

SOB
HEY!!
AW, LISTEN, COME WITH ME AND WE'LL--

GREAT-- ANOTHER CAT KICKER...
I SAID HEY!!

GET UP NOW!

?
GET GOIN'!
BAKERY

DOWN TO THE BAKERY, DOWN--DOWN!!

WAIT!!

YOU'RE TOO FAT FOR THIS. WHAT ARE YOU-- ONE OF THOSE UNDERCOVER INSPECTORS?

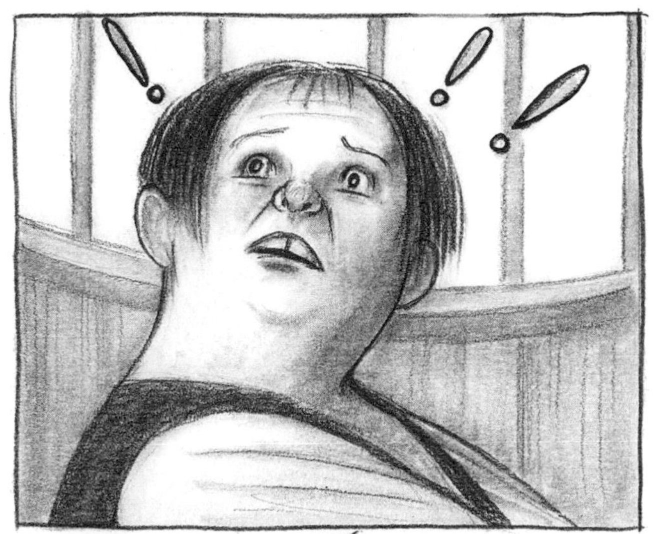
! ! !

WHAT? WHAT IS IT?!
I'LL KILL YOU WITH MY BARE HANDS!

I'VE... SEEN... YOUR DREAM...

MY WHAT?? GET DOWN THERE-- NOW!

DID THE BOUNCERS MENTION ME? DID THEY RECEIVE MY RÉSUMÉ?
?

YOU SAW HOW I HANDLED THAT CATTLE PROD! I'M A BORN LEADER.

THEY THINK THEY KNOW POWER--HA! THEY HAVE NO IDEA.

BRAINLESS, ENTITLED BASTARDS! COME ON! THE BAKERY'S THROUGH HERE..

CAF
SOB
BAR
SOB!
"The World in a Bite"

DO YOU KNOW HOW I GOT THIS CROWN?

ISN'T IT A TIARA, PRIMUS?

NOT WHEN *I'M* WEARING IT...
YESSIR.
SORRY, SIR...

I ACQUIRED IT FROM A WHORE THIS MORNING. SHE SAID THAT MR. BISCUIT HAD BEEN HER "DEAR, DEAR FRIEND"...

THE PETTY THIEF CLAIMED IT WAS A GIFT FROM HIM!

"THAT'S HIS CROWN YOU STOLE!" I SAID. SHE DENIED IT, OF COURSE...

...SO I TOOK HER UP TO THE BRIDGE...

"I'M NOT A JUMPER!" SHE SAID. I TOLD HER SHE WOULDN'T HAVE TO JUMP.

THEN I "GAVE HER THE SCARF" AND DUMPED HER OVER, SIMPLE AND NEAT.

TODAY WE USE OUR SCARVES FOR THEIR TRUE PURPOSE, UNDERSTAND?
YESSIR!

AM I NOT THE ONE LEADER?
OH YESSIR!

?!
CRASH

GIVE IT TO ME!
NO!!!

EASY, FOLKS! VIOLENCE IS NOT THE ANSWER.
SHOW HIM!

WHAT IS IT?
IT CAME OUTA THE DOWNSPOUT.

A WADDED UP NOTE...
THE IDIOT TRIED TO EAT IT! THOUGHT IT WAS A BISCUIT!

HMMM... TOO MANY WORDS. IT CAN'T BE IMPORTANT...

LOOK! ANOTHER ONE!!
PFFFT

LET ME EAT IT!
EASY, FELLA..
LOOK AT THAT...!

IT SAYS THE SAME THING AS THE OTHER ONE...
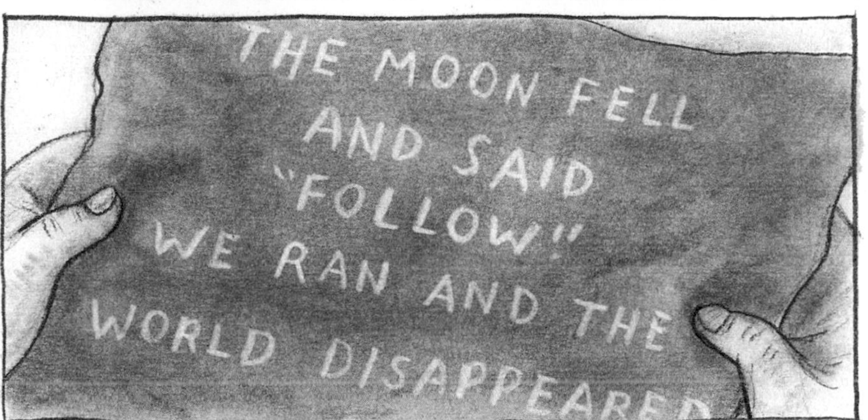
THE MOON FELL AND SAID "FOLLOW!" WE RAN AND THE WORLD DISAPPEARED

WHAT DOES IT MEAN?
WHAT DO YOU *MEAN* "WHAT DOES IT MEAN?"?!

IT'S **CODE**, YOU FOOL! ***SEDITIOUS CODE!!*** FIND THE **SOURCE**!

BAKERY
FOLLOW ME CLOSELY...

YOU'D BETTER KNOW HOW TO WORK HARD AND PERFECTLY...

BISCUIT DEMAND IS AT AN ALL-TIME HIGH...

UP THERE'S THE MIXER, THEN YOU GOT THE EXTRUDER, THE FORMING CYLINDER, BUT YOU CAN FORGET ABOUT THAT JOB...

THIS PLACE IS A WELL-OILED MACHINE AND YOU CAN THANK *ME* FOR THAT.

MICKEY! SWEEP UP THE DAMNED LUNCHROOM!
YEAH, YEAH...

AND TIGHTEN THE BOLTS ON THE BACKUP MIXER NOW!
THAT'S NOT MY FAULT! PIT MUST'VE SABOTAGED IT.
FIX IT ANYWAY!!

STOP STARING AT THE OVEN CREW! THAT'S A CUSHY JOB YOU'LL NEVER HAVE..

AND THE COOLING RACKS? THAT'S AN ELITE POSITION. DON'T EVEN TRY...

NOW HERE'S WHERE IT ALL HAPPENS...

THIS HERE'S THE PRINTER. IT GETS THE NEWS DIRECT FROM THE GREAT ANTENNA!

...PRINTS THE NEWS RIGHT ONTO THE BISCUITS.
CRAVE APE

THAT KNOWLEDGE IS REAL AND IMPORTANT AND WE MAKE IT HAPPEN.

?
WHAT ARE YOUR SKILLS, ASSUMING YOU HAVE ANY?

I... I CAN CARRY THINGS... AND PEOPLE...
THAT'S IT?!

PORTLY
CASABA
FAT JACKASS OOZES CALAMITY
SINISTER JACKASS
UNNATURAL STENCH PERVERTS

MR.MICKEY, I SEE A LOT OF JACKASSES. IS THE PRINTER STUCK?
??!

OF COURSE NOT! THE WORLD IS STUCK!!

?!
NOW GET AWAY FROM THERE! ONLY THE BLIND ARE ALLOWED TO SEE THOSE!

I'VE COME HERE TO GET SMOKE STICKS.
SMOKE STICKS?

YES. MY FRIEND OLD LLOYD NEEDS THEM OR HE'LL DIE.

THEY SIPHON OUT HIS INNER SMOKE.

?

OH WOW, OH BOY-- SO THIS IS HOW THE BOUNCERS RUB MY FACE IN IT, SENDING ME A MORON WITH A FAIRY TALE!

MR. MICKEY, I AM NOT A MORON.

FINE--THEN MAKE YOURSELF USEFUL!

YOU SHOULD BE BOWING TO ME. I KNOW MORE THAN ANYONE HERE, AND I HAVE THE KEYS TO EVERY LOCK.

SINCE YOU'RE A MORON I'LL SPILL A FEW FACTS YOU AIN'T BRAINY ENOUGH TO REPEAT...

VAULT 1
VAULT 12
THESE ARE THE VAULTS, FULL OF THE GOODS PEOPLE TRADED FOR THE BISCUITS.
I'VE WATCHED BOUNCERS COME THROUGH HERE, FULL OF DESIRES.

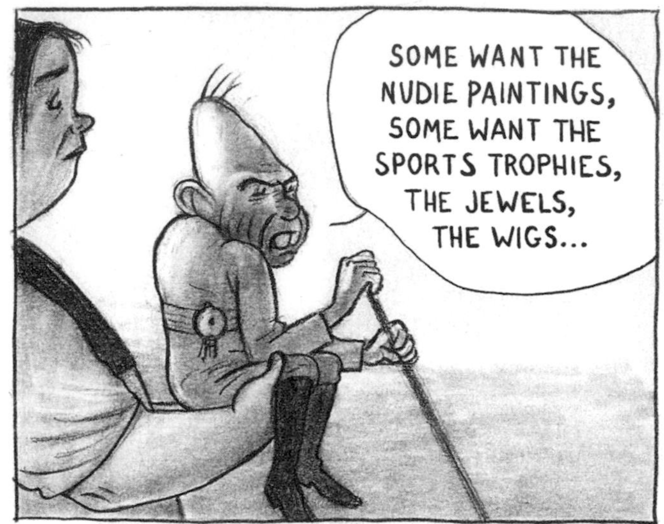
SOME WANT THE NUDIE PAINTINGS, SOME WANT THE SPORTS TROPHIES, THE JEWELS, THE WIGS...

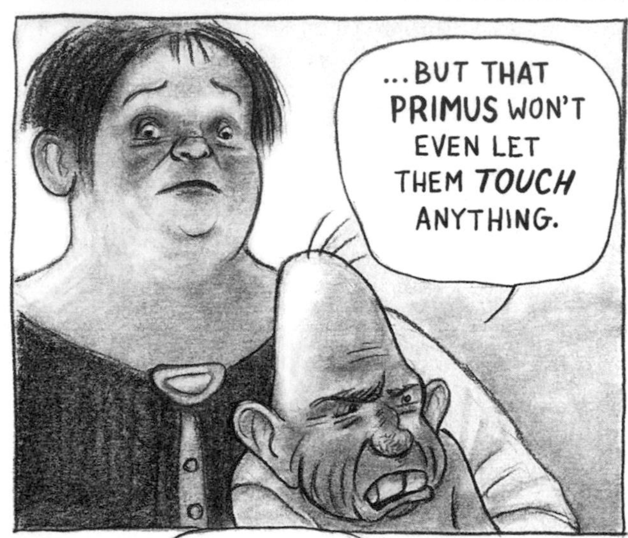
...BUT THAT PRIMUS WON'T EVEN LET THEM *TOUCH* ANYTHING.

BOUNCERS GET HIGH FROM TAKING OTHER FOLKS' THINGS, BUT THERE'S MORE TO LIFE. YOU GOTTA KNOW HOW TO READ THE PATTERNS IN THOSE PILES--WHAT PEOPLE *DESIRE*, WHAT THEY FEAR LOSING...

IF I KNOW A MAN'S CRAVINGS I CAN ENGINEER HIS DEPRIVATION.
EVEN *PRIMUS'S*...

PRIMUS! PFFFT. HE ONLY *THINKS* HE'S HUMILIATING ME. I WILL BREAK HIM IN HALF...
WHY DID YOU STOP? ARE YOU AN INSPECTOR? PLEASE!-- I *NEED* THIS JOB...

I KNOW A GUY... HE CAN FIND YOUR MAGICAL SMOKE STICKS...

HE KEEPS TRACK OF EVERYTHING THAT'S BEEN BROUGHT HERE.

THANK YOU.
YEAH, YEAH...

BEFORE I LET YOU IN...
...REMEMBER OUR DEAL...

WHAT DEAL?

DON'T BE COY WITH ME! YOU'RE FAT! YOU HAVE INFLUENCE, AND YOU'RE GOING TO GET ME A MEETING WITH THE BOUNCERS!

HE'S IN THERE. THE NAME'S "PIT". HURRY UP!
INVENTORY

MR. PIT?
HELLO! I'LL BE JUST A MOMENT.

?
FEEL FREE TO PICK SOME FOREST PLUMS IF YOU'RE HUNGRY.

THANK YOU.

I KNOW THIS FRUIT.

THERE'S AN OLD WIVE'S TALE...THAT IF YOU EAT TOO MUCH OF IT YOU'LL FIND YOURSELF STUCK LONGING FOR THE PAST...

OR...

...THE *FUTURE.*

AHHH--YES! A BACKWARDS NOSTALGIA. IT CAN HAVE THAT EFFECT, TOO.

THERE'S ONLY ONE TREE OF THIS KIND IN THE CITY.

THANK YOU.
WHY DON'T YOU TAKE THE PIT-- AS A MEMENTO!

MR. PIT, DO YOU HAVE SMOKE STICKS? A FRIEND OF MINE NEEDS THEM BADLY.

OH YES, I HAVE THEM, BUT THE QUESTION IS WHERE! INVENTORY HAS QUADRUPLED IN THE LAST WEEK! A THOUSAND NEW BOXES TO SORT.

I...I CAN HELP YOU.
OH--THAT WOULD BE WONDERFUL!

RIGHT, THEN. THROUGH HERE...

WHERE DID YOU SAY YOU WERE FROM?
I... DIDN'T.
OH, WELL, IT'S JUST THAT...

...YOU HAVE A CERTAIN... PULL ABOUT YOU. I DON'T DOUBT YOU COULD ENTER A WHIRLWIND OF RUBBLE AND SOMEHOW MAKE IT ORDERLY.
YOU OUGHT TO WORK HERE...

MR. PIT!–MR. PIT!!
YES, MICKEY, WHAT IS IT?

OH GOSH!–THEY NEED YOU OUT AT THE DOCKS! A NEW LOAD'S JUST ARRIVED!

OH... I...I SEE...

THE DOCKS, YOU SAY?
YESSIR! IT WAS TOO BIG FOR THE ELEVATOR...

ALL RIGHT, MICKEY...

...I SHALL ATTEND TO IT...

RIGHT OUT THERE, MR. PIT! THEY'RE WAITING FOR YOU...

?.?.
THAT'S IT, SIR, THROUGH THERE...

AW, HECK, NO SHIPMENT! MY MISTAKE...
AH...AH..

WHAT'S THE MATTER WITH HIM?
SHHHH! WATCH..

AH...AHHH..

AH--AH--AAHHHAHHAAHAAHHAH

CHOOOOO
HA, HA!

HA HA HA--HE'S--HA HA--HE'S ALLERGIC TO THE SKY, "THE ORBS" HE SAYS!!

'CAUSE "ONCE UPON A TIME" THE MOON FELL TO THE GROUND AND THE WORLD ENDED! ISN'T THAT WHAT YOU SAID, PIT?
HA HA HA

THE MOON.. FELL?
I... I'M SO SORRY...
ISN'T THAT HOW YOU GOT YOUR CUSHY INDOOR JOB, YOU LAZY GRUB?!
HA HA HA HA HA HA...

ARE YOU ALL RIGHT, MR. PIT? HOW CAN I HELP YOU?

I'M AFRAID NO ONE CAN HELP ME.

DON'T BLAME MICKEY. MY PROBLEM IS NOT WITH HIM...

... IT IS WITH THE LONG-AGO...

A MOON...
...FELL! HA, HA, HA!! NEVER GETS OLD...

WHAT A PATHETIC, LAZY, NO-GOOD GRUB! HA, HA, HEH, HA-- SO EASY TO CONTROL!
HA
HA
HA HA

HA
HA
HA
SO GULLIBLE!
HA

WHERE ARE YOU GOING?? GET BACK TO WORK!
I HAVE TO LEAVE HERE...

YOU'RE GOING TO MAKE ME LOOK BAD!

I'VE STAYED TOO LONG. I KNOW TOO MUCH.

YOU KNOW NOTHING! WE HAD A DEAL!!
TAKE ME TO THE BOUNCERS!

LET ME GO, SIR...
YOU'LL GO WHEN I SAY SO!
PLEASE... TAKE ME TO THE BOUNCERS.
PLEASE...
I'LL LOCK THEM IN THE VAULTS AND GAS THEM!

YOU WANT TO TRAP THE BOUNCERS AND KILL THEM.

WHA?? HOW DID YOU KNOW MY PLAN?

NOBODY KNOWS THAT--I KEEP IT IN MY HEAD!
SOME DREAMS SHOULD STAY DREAMS...

I'M SORRY FOR YOU, MR. PIT..

I WISH I COULD HELP YOU.

?
?

I CAN'T HELP ANYONE...

???
PFFFT

THE MOON FELL
AND SAID
"FOLLOW."
WE RAN AND THE
WORLD DISAPPEARED

THE MOON FELL..

THIS IS MR. PIT'S STORY...

THE MOON SAID "FOLLOW."

I SAW THIS IN THE FJORD!

FOLLOW!

WHAT DOES IT *MEAN,* MR. PIT?

P--PUH.. PLEASE...

MUH, MAY I READ IT?

THUH-- TH-- THEY'VE B--BEEN DROPPING OUT OF DRAINPIPES ALL OVER TUH-TOWN..

I'M ...MMM NOT FUH **FAST** ENOUGH TO GUH **GET** TO TH-THEM..

B--B-BUT, EVERYONE S--SAYS, **SAAAYS...**

...TH--THEY ARE... **TRUE.** THEY... ARE **WONDERFUL.**

TRUE?

WOULDN'T YOU PREFER A BISCUIT?
OH, NO...NO...

...N--NOT ANYMORE.

!!

WHERE'D THAT MORON GO?

???
PFFFT

"THE MOON FELL"?! DAMN YOU, PIT!!

WELL, WELL, WELL...

HELLO, FRIEND.
PLEASE, HAND OVER THE SEDITIOUS NOTE...
...AND RETURN TO YOUR BISCUIT EATING.

FRIEND?? BISCUIT EATING?! AFTER ALL THIS TIME YOU DON'T KNOW WHO I AM??

THE BISCUIT BAKERY IS A WELL-OILED MACHINE AND YOU'RE LOOKING AT THE OIL!!

I KNOW EXACTLY WHO'S BEHIND THIS NOTE!

AND I WILL SPEAK TO NO ONE BUT YOUR COMMANDING OFFICER, IS THAT CLEAR?

??

YOU BELIEVE HIM?
YEAH.
YOU TRUST HIM?
DOES IT MATTER?

THOSE NOTES ARE DROPPING EVERYWHERE...
...AND IF THE BISCUITS GO UNDER...
...SO DO WE.

IT CAME OUT OF HERE.

A MOON FELL...

IS THAT REAL?
?

ABNORMAL TREADMILL
UNEXPLAIN DANDRUFF
DISASTE
MUTILATES JACKASS

THEY'VE STOPPED READING THE BISCUITS..

?!
NO--NO!
STAY AWAY FROM THE PAPERS!
NO! NO!
GET BACK TO THE BISCUITS!

?!!
NO...

LOOK AT ME!

YOU PUSHED US TO DO THIS!

COUGH
COUGH

HOW DARE YOU?

ENOUGH!

IN THE DARK YOU COULD'VE BEEN HANDSOME...

...BUT YOUR UGLY VOICE WOULD DELIGHT IN HUMILIATING ME.

WATCH AND LEARN, BROTHERS.
YESSIR!

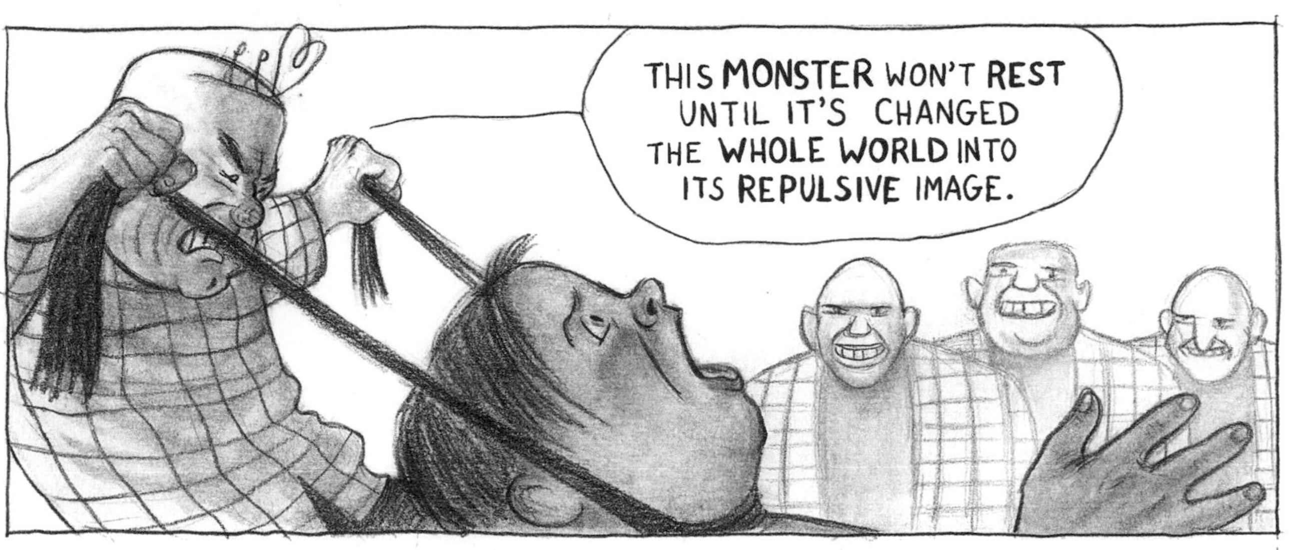
THIS MONSTER WON'T REST UNTIL IT'S CHANGED THE WHOLE WORLD INTO ITS REPULSIVE IMAGE.

I WANT NO SUCH THING!

I WANT PEOPLE TO DREAM.

I WANT PEOPLE TO DREAM!!

WITHOUT DREAMS... WE ARE LOST.

ARE YOU THE KING NOW, YOU--YOU CHICKEN SUCKLER?

??!?

HERE IS YOUR KINGDOM!

IF YOU KEEP EVEN ONE MORE PERSON FROM DREAMING...

...I WILL TAKE YOU APART.

PSSSST!

FOLLOW ME UP HERE...

DON'T WORRY, NO ONE WILL SEE US, NOT *HERE*...

THEY DON'T SEE WHAT THEY DON'T REMEMBER.

EVERYONE USED TO **PICNIC** UP HERE, BUT THAT WAS BEFORE THE **BISCUITS**...

I'M GLAD TO SEE YOU AGAIN.
THAT MAKES **TWO** OF US.

I DON'T LIKE THIS **CITY**.

I DON'T LIKE WHAT I'VE BECOME HERE.
?

THEN WHY DID YOU COME?

FOR THE SMOKE STICKS... THEY SIPHON OUT A PERSON'S INNER SMOKE.
WHO TOLD YOU *THAT?*
THE MAN WHO SENT ME HERE.

YOU ARE ONE SURPRISE AFTER ANOTHER...

WHAT ELSE DID THE MAN TELL YOU?

HE SAID THAT IF HE DIDN'T GET THEM HE'D DIE.
HE'LL DIE ANYWAY! EVERYONE DOES.

WOULD YOU MIND CARRYING ME? THE NEXT THOUSAND STEPS ARE STEEP.

DON'T BE DISCOURAGED.
I KNOW THINGS...

...AND I KNOW SOMEONE WHO'LL HELP YOU...

...IN THERE.

THANK YOU FOR TRUSTING ME.

??!
WHERE IS HE??

ZELDA DEAR, HOW ARE YOU?

HOW DO YOU THINK?! MISERY-- MISERY!

WHERE IS HE? WHY DIDN'T HE BRING ME MY TREAT? WHY HASN'T HE HELD ME TODAY?

ZELDA, HE'S--
NO!! HE TOLD ME THERE WAS NOTHING BEYOND THE SENSES! SO HE CANNOT BE DEAD!

I DON'T BELIEVE HE'S DEAD, THEREFORE HE IS NOT.

ZELDA, YOU'RE STANDING IN YOUR PEE...
I DON'T CARE!

WHERE IS HE?
SOB
SOB
SOB
WELCOME TO THE CEMETERY.

?

WHAT ARE THESE?

HAVEN'T YOU EVER SEEN EPITAPHS?
NO.
THEY'RE SO TRUTHFUL...
...LIKE...*DREAMS*...
YES, I SUPPOSE...

PLAYED ACCORDION IN FIVE DIFFERENT BANDS. THE LADIES LOVED ME.
ALMOST BECAME AN OPERA SINGER. ALMOST BECAME MANY THINGS.
PARALYSIS MADE ME A BETTER FLORIST.
NEVER SAID MUCH. WHY START NOW?
ALL MY OFFSPRING DISAPPOINTED ME. LEFT MY MONEY TO THE DOG
OUTLIVED THREE HUSBANDS NOT MY
OPEN
THIRTY GRANDCHILDREN, GREAT GRAND-CHILDREN
I SOLD LIQUOR. ALWAYS SMILED. HAD NOT ONE ENEMY.
I DELIVERED SOUP WITH THE SLED, ON THE FROZEN RIVER. SAVED A BOY'S LIFE THERE.
ALL THE KIDS PLAYED IN
YARD.
WE WERE IMMIGRANTS. DOCTORS. HAPPY. DIED ONE DAY APART.
ONCE I BREATHED MY OWN STORY. NOW IT BREATHES

I THOUGHT YOU MIGHT LIKE THIS PLACE.

YES. I DO.

IT REMINDS ME OF HOME.

THERE IT IS AGAIN!

THE MOON FELL AND SAID "FOLLOW."
WE RAN AND THE WORLD DISAPPEARED.

I'VE SEEN THAT STORY!
HAVE YOU?

SIT. I'VE BEEN MEANING TO ASK YOU SOMETHING...

WOULD YOU--
--BETTY! IS THAT YOU?

YES, DEAR!

HOW HAVE OUR LITTLE NOTES BEEN RECEIVED?
JUST AS YOU PREDICTED...

ALL OVER THE CITY THEY'RE ABANDONING THE BISCUITS.

THOSE EPITAPHS ARE WINNING THEIR ATTENTION.
AS IT SHOULD BE.
3RD AVENUE
EAST PLAZA

THE BOUNCERS ARE FIGHTING IT.
OF COURSE.
SCRUNCH
LIBRARY
MUSEUM
3RD AVENUE
EAST PLAZA

WE'RE DOING THE RIGHT THING, DEAR.
WHOOSH
3RD AVENUE
EAST PLAZA

THAT'S VIOLET, MY OLD LADY.

THE EPITAPHS ON THESE WALLS-- SHE'S MADE RUBBINGS OF THEM AND IS SENDING THEM DOWN TO THE CITY.

THERE'S A WHOLE NETWORK OF FALSE DRAINPIPES. THEY WERE USED DURING THE WAR TO SEND DISPATCHES.
!

VIOLET KNOWS ALL ABOUT THAT... SHE KNOWS A LOT OF THINGS...

NO ONE IN THE CITY REMEMBERS THE WAR, OR THE DEAD, OR THIS PLACE.

ZELDA DEAR, WHAT IS IT?

WHAT DO YOU THINK??? I AM MISERABLE... MISERABLE!

WHERE IS HE??
HE-- HE CANNOT BE DEAD!

NO ONE WILL LOVE ME LIKE THAT AGAIN...

NOT TRUE, ZELDA.
OH, PLEASE! YOU CANNOT KNOW MY PAIN...
BETTY?!

HAVE YOU FOUND A NEW FRIEND?
YES, DEAR.
HELLO.

AND WHAT IS YOUR NAME?
EARTHA.

EARTHA! A BEAUTIFUL NAME! AND A BEAUTIFUL, HONEST FACE...

YOU'RE NOT NATIVE TO HERE, ARE YOU?
NO, MA'AM.
I'M FROM... THE COUNTRY.

STRANGE...THERE'S SOMETHING SO... FAMILIAR ABOUT YOU. WOULDN'T YOU AGREE, BETTY?
YES, VIOLET.

YOUR HAT PIN...
YES?

IT LOOKS JUST LIKE THIS PIT.

AH--!

WOULD YOU LOOK AT THAT, BETTY?! I'VE NEVER SEEN ANOTHER OF THESE UNTIL NOW!

WHEREVER DID YOU GET IT, EARTHA?
WELL, A FELLOW IN THE BAKERY--

EXCUSE ME -- MIGHT I FINISH WHAT I'VE BEEN TRYING TO SAY? THERE'S NO GETTING AROUND THIS, VIOLET...

OF COURSE, DEAR.
?

HOW DO I BEGIN... YOU SEE, EVER SINCE WE RETURNED TO THE CITY LAST WEEK...

I'VE BEEN SEEKING A NEW-- OH, IT ALL SOUNDS SO HEARTLESS NOW!

THEN I'LL SAY IT: EARTHA, DEAR, BETTY NEEDS A NEW COMPANION AND SHE'S CHOSEN YOU.

IT'S PERFECTLY UNDERSTANDABLE...
?
SOB

I'M ALWAYS TRAVELING, BUT MY DEAR OLD FRIEND IS READY FOR A QUIET RETIREMENT IN THE COUNTRY.

AND I WILL MISS HER BEYOND MEASURE.

OOOOOH...
SOB

SHE LIKES TO BE HELD THIS WAY.
THERE, THERE, DEAR.
SOB

NORMALLY I'D BE OF BETTER CHEER...
SOB

...BUT BETWEEN DADDY'S DEATH LAST WEEK, AND NOW BETTY'S LEAVE-TAKING...
SOB!
SOB

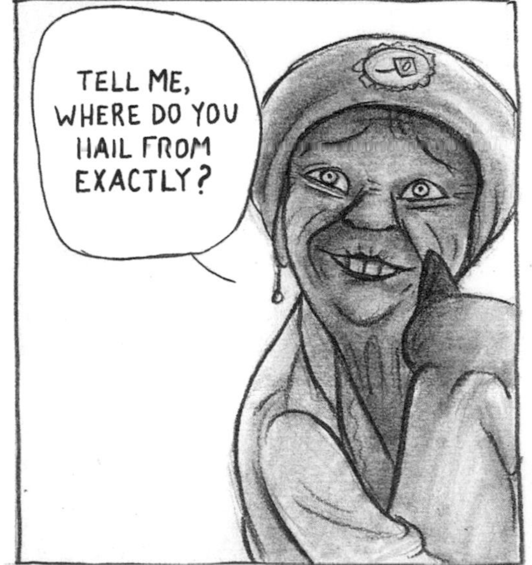
TELL ME, WHERE DO YOU HAIL FROM EXACTLY?

MY *HOME*? I...I CAN'T SAY...

OH. WELL, CAN YOU TELL ME WHAT YOU *DO* THERE? FOR A LIVING?

YES. I CARRY PEOPLE... AND COLLECT SHADOWS...

COLLECTING SHADOWS! THAT SOUNDS LIKE IMPORTANT WORK.
SOB

ALL RIGHT, DEAR ONE...
SOB

LET'S LOOK OUT AT THE LAKE... AND BREATHE...
GOOD.

YOU'VE SEEN THE SHRINES TO THE SMILING BALD MAN?
YES.

ALL THOSE BOUNCERS DRESS JUST LIKE HIM.

YES, WELL MR. BISCUIT IS--WAS--MY FATHER...

HE CANNOT BE DEAD!!

I REFUSE TO BELIEVE IT!!
OH ZELDA..

BORN:
DIED:
IT'S BEEN ONLY A WEEK, DEAR. WE ALL MOURN HIM.
SOB

MUMMY AND DADDY STARTED THE "EDIBLE NEWS" BUSINESS.

THEY'D BEEN ORDINARY BAKERS, SUCCESSFUL, BUT NOT WEALTHY. THEN THE WAR BROKE OUT...

MIND YOU, IT NEVER REACHED THIS WELL-GUARDED CITY...
SOB.

BUT IT SCRATCHED AND HISSED AT THE BORDER, AND THE PEOPLE HERE BREATHED DREAD.

MUMMY VOLUNTEERED UP HERE AT THE DISPATCH POST, WHILE DADDY RAN THE BAKERY DOWN AT THE CANAL...

...AND HE OBSERVED THAT WHENEVER DISPATCHES CAME DOWN PEOPLE'S DREAD INCREASED, ALONG WITH PASTRY SALES.
YOU SMELL GOOD.

THE WAR ENDED, BUT NOT THE CRAVING FOR DREAD AND PASTRY, SO MUMMY AND DADDY COMBINED BOTH AND GOT RICH. DADDY BECAME "MR. BISCUIT"...
WHILE MUMMY EXPANDED THE BAKERY AND DESIGNED THE "GREAT ANTENNA."

SHE DIED YEARS AGO. I WAS ABROAD AT THE TIME. DADDY INSISTED I STAY AWAY, THAT HE NEEDED TO MOURN ALONE. SO I WAITED... AND WAITED.
SCUIT

...AND THAT WAS WHEN ALL THE TROUBLE STARTED.

WITH MUMMY GONE DADDY COULDN'T FIND HIMSELF, SO HE DECIDED TO BANISH ALL MEMORY OF HER...

...AND YOUNG PRIMUS SUDDENLY STEPPED IN AND OFFERED HIS DUBIOUS SERVICES, RECRUITING "BOUNCERS"...
BOUNCERS..
THAT WORTHLESS, NO-GOOD LOT OF CAT KICKERS!
Nooo

IN THOSE LOYAL BOYS DADDY COULD SEE HIMSELF EVERYWHERE. THEY WERE HIS PLAID REFLECTIONS, DRESSED BY PRIMUS, NOW SECURELY UNDER DADDY'S WING.
THE BLOATED, MORALIZING HYENA!!
NOOO

"MEANING IS A PHANTOM! CONNECTION IS AN ILLUSION! I WILL NEVER, EVER TOUCH HER AGAIN!"

PRIMUS TOOK A WIDOWER'S LAMENT AND MADE IT INTO A SALESMAN'S CREED.

I SAW HIM KILL A WOMAN AND STEAL HER TIARA! AND WHY? BECAUSE SHE WAS THE ONE TO TELL HIM THAT YOUR FATHER HAD DIED.
PLEASE..

HE DOESN'T UNDERSTAND THOSE WORDS --OR ANY WORDS!-- ONLY THE EFFECT THEY HAVE ON WEAKENED PEOPLE...
NO

HE SEPARATES THEM FROM THEIR HOMES-- FROM EACH OTHER!
NO!

!
NOOOOOO!
?!

DON'T YOU UNDERSTAND?

HUMANS NEVER NEEDED BISCUITS TO AVOID EACH OTHER.

MR. BISCUIT WAS GOOD TO ME. HE LOOKED ME IN THE EYES.

HE LISTENED TO ME! HE TOLD ME HE LOVED ME! EVERY DAY HE SAID IT!

HE ALWAYS HAD A JOKE FOR ME, AND A TREAT IF I LAUGHED!

NO ONE WILL EVER LOVE ME LIKE THAT AGAIN!
OH ZELDA...

NOT TRUE, DEAR...

SOB
SOB
NOT TRUE.

LAP, LAP, LAP.

LET US LEAVE ZELDA IN PEACE AWHILE.

I WANT TO TELL YOU BOTH HOW DADDY DIED.

ZELDA DOESN'T KNOW, AND FOR NOW THINGS MUST STAY THAT WAY. HE WAS HER WHOLE WORLD, AFTER ALL...

BUT WHAT A GOOD DEATH IT WAS!

IT ALL BEGAN WHILE HE WAS WALKING TO HIS PRIVATE BORDELLO.
IT WASN'T MUCH OF A BORDELLO ANYMORE. DADDY'S LADY FRIENDS HAD BECOME HIS ACCOUNTANTS AND SUPPLY MANAGERS. THE BAKERY COULDN'T RUN WITHOUT THEM.
DADDY HAD BAKED HIMSELF A CAKE AND WAS GOING THERE TO CELEBRATE HIS BIRTHDAY...

...WHEN HE SLIPPED ON A SLUG AND HIT HIS HEAD ON A STATUE OF HIS HEAD.

ALERT VIOLET AT ONCE!
I'LL GO AND BREAK THE NEWS TO PRIMUS.
PRIMUS? ARE YOU SURE?

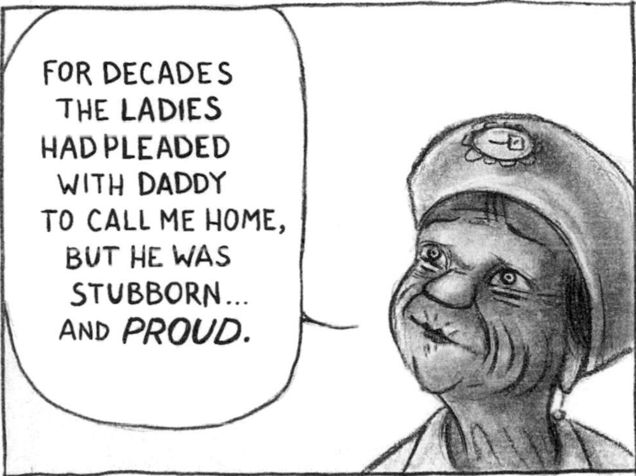
FOR DECADES THE LADIES HAD PLEADED WITH DADDY TO CALL ME HOME, BUT HE WAS STUBBORN... AND PROUD.

THANKFULLY HE LINGERED LONG ENOUGH FOR ME TO RETURN...
I'LL LEAVE YOU TWO ALONE.

HELLO
HE SAID, THEN OBSERVED:
YOU'RE VERY OLD..
AND I LAUGHED.
YES...OF COURSE...AGE IS...WHAT... TIME... DOES...
OF COURSE I AM!

AND, FOR THE FIRST TIME IN YEARS, DADDY SMILED HIS FAMOUS "MR. BISCUIT" SMILE.
SIT WITH ME A WHILE... I...I HAVE S--SOMETHING TO TELL YOU...

YOUR MUMMY... USED TO SAY THAT BELIEFS WERE LIKE PARASITES... THEY COULD TAKE YOU OVER, UNAWARES...

SHE WAS MY ROCK! WHEN SHE DIED--OH!--TO THINK I WOULD NEVER, EVER TOUCH HER AGAIN! IT TURNED ME MAD! AND MEAN...

SHE MADE ME PROMISE TO TELL YOU SOMETHING...
WHAT, DADDY?
THE TRUTH!

SHE ALWAYS SAID WE WERE IGNORING OURSELVES, WHERE WE'D BEEN, WHERE WE WERE GOING... THAT ANY INVADER COULD JUST WIPE US OFF OUR SURFACE AND FIND NOTHING UNDERNEATH...
OH--OH! I'VE MADE THIS CITY ROT! CAUGHT UP WITH STUPID IDEAS... PEOPLE DON'T EVEN DREAM ANYMORE!! ALL CYNICS! YOU HAVE TO EARN THAT RIGHT!
COUGH, COUGH..
DADDY, PLEASE..

CALM DOWN...

WHAT DID YOU DO... ALL THOSE YEARS AWAY?

I TRAVELED. I HELPED PEOPLE, AND THEY HELPED ME.
WERE THERE WARS?
YES, BUT MOSTLY PEACE.
WELL, WELL, IS THAT A FACT?!

YOU SHOULD KNOW, DADDY! YOU GOT THE NEWS FROM EVERYWHERE AT EVERY MOMENT!

NO I DIDN'T-- NOBODY DID! THE ANTENNA'S A FAKE! THAT'S WHAT MUMMY WANTED ME TO TELL YOU...

FAKE? BUT THE BISCUIT NEWS..?
PFFFT! JUMBLED WORDS STAMPED ONTO PASTRY.

MUMMY AND I JUST WANTED TO SELL MORE BISCUITS! IT GOT A LITTLE OUT OF HAND...

???

??!
HA HA HA HA HA

HA HA HA HA HA HA HA

THEY THINK THEY KNOW THE WORLD! HOW CAN YOU KNOW THE WORLD IF YOU DON'T KNOW YOURSELF?

TEAR IT ALL DOWN, SWEET GIRL! FIND A WAY! MAKE US PROUD!
I WILL, DADDY.

THEY NEED THEIR DREAMS BACK! THEIR OWN QUIET THOUGHTS...
OH... LOOK... THERE'S YOUR MUMMY, LAUGHING WITH... US....... OH...

FOR YEARS DADDY TURNED A BLIND EYE TO PRIMUS'S SCHEMING.
...BECAUSE HE DIDN'T WANT TO BE ALONE...
PRIMUS-UGH!

NEVER MIND ABOUT HIM, BETTY. HE HAS NO HOLD ON US.
I'LL SEND DOWN EVERY EPITAPH HERE--TRUE STORIES...

... AND THAT WILL BRING EVERYONE BACK TO THEIR SENSES.

THE MOON FELL AND SAID "FOLLOW!" WE RAN AND THE WORLD DISAPPEARED.

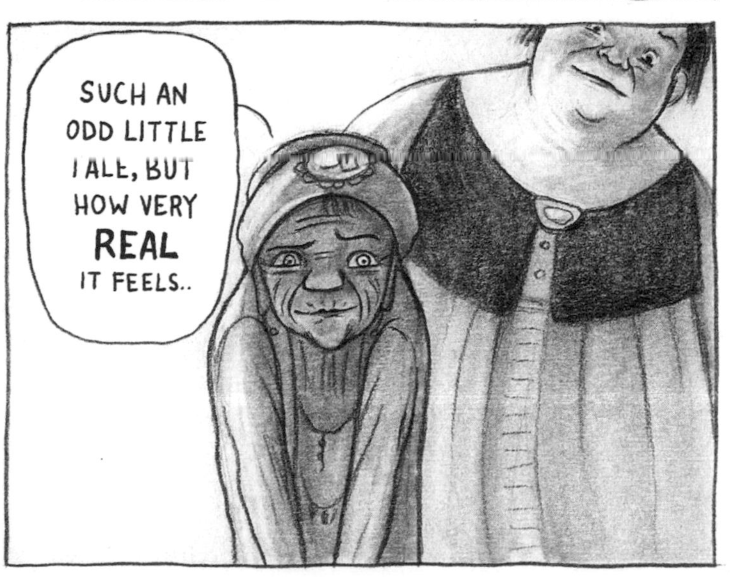
SUCH AN ODD LITTLE TALE, BUT HOW VERY REAL IT FEELS..

Eartha felt light-headed,
a stranger to ordinary
time and space.

Had it been only hours ago
that she'd saved a child's
dream from a crashing moon?
That a little wisp of thought
had held her tightly by the neck?

Was that child the woman who
stood before her?

Eartha wondered if Violet
had meant to call her across
the sea with this borrowed vision,
and why the same dream
had condemned Mr. Pit
to a hermit's life.

I KNOW YOU'LL CARE FOR HER WELL.
YES, I WILL.

WHAT ABOUT *YOU*, VIOLET?
BETTY, I KNOW EVERY WAY OUT OF THIS CITY...

AND WHEN THE LAST BISCUIT CRUMBLES I'LL LEAVE, UNNOTICED.

NOW GO AND ENJOY YOUR RETIREMENT IN THE COUNTRY.

I TRAVEL EVERYWHERE, YOU KNOW...

SO WHEN YOU REMEMBER WHERE YOU'RE FROM I JUST MIGHT COME FOR A VISIT.

TAKE CARE, DEAR ONES, AND KEEP CLEAR OF THE BOUNCERS.

FOR THEM THE WORLD IS ENDING. THEY'LL BE MOST VIOLENT.
THANK YOU, VIOLET...
FOR EVERYTHING.

GOODBYE FOR NOW, LOVE.

SOB.

Eartha and Betty made their way to a new life...
...while Primus and the Bouncers were busily preserving City order...
GENTLEMEN!
BAKERY
...allowing Mickey to lead them to a "traitor."

FOLLOW ME TO THE SOURCE OF THOSE SEDITIOUS "MOON" MISSIVES...

AND YOU WILL FINALLY UNDERSTAND JUST HOW MUCH YOU NEED ME IN YOUR RANKS. I WILL EXPAND OUR REACH IMMEASURABLY, INTO THE FUTURE AND BEYOND.

HONORABLE BROTHER! BEFORE YOU LEAD US DOWN TO THE BAKERY WE'LL NEED A PLAN, IN CASE WE BECOME SEPARATED.
!

WHY, BROTHER PRIMUS, I AM IMPRESSED THAT YOU ARE WILLING TO DISCUSS STRATEGY.

IF NEED BE WE SHOULD RE-ASSEMBLE AT THE THIRD SORTING BELT. BEYOND IT, PAST THE SHIPPING ESCALATORS, IS THE DOOR TO THE INVENTORY CORRIDOR, AS YOU WELL KNOW.

HIS IS THE EASTERN-MOST OFFICE, PAST THE EIGHTH STORAGE VAULT. HE IS A SCRAWNY, PROUD FELLOW WITH AN UNKEMPT BEARD AND AN ALLERGY TO SUN AND MOON, A LOWLY GRUB WHO REVEALS HIS TREACHERY WITH EVERY SNEEZE...
OF COURSE.

WHAT'S MORE, HE IS COLLABORATING WITH THE ENORMOUS SHE-BUMPKIN THAT YOU SENT TO ME ONLY HOURS AGO.
!
THE... SHE-BUMPKIN?

SHE ATTEMPTED TO INTIMIDATE ME BY PRETENDING TO READ MY MIND. AN UTTER FAILURE, OF COURSE.
OF COURSE.

DOES YOUR SMILE FALTER, BRAVE LAD?
NO, SIR-- I... AM SIMPLY... OVERCOME.

BE NOT OVERCOME. KNOW YOUR ORDERS AND FOLLOW ME.

THIS IS OUR FINEST HOUR!

ONWARD AND DOWNWARD, MEN!

YESSIR!!

ONWARD AND DOWNWARD...

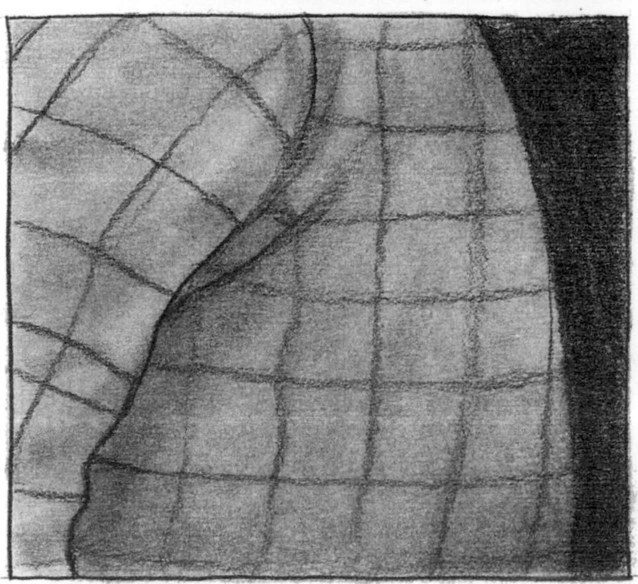

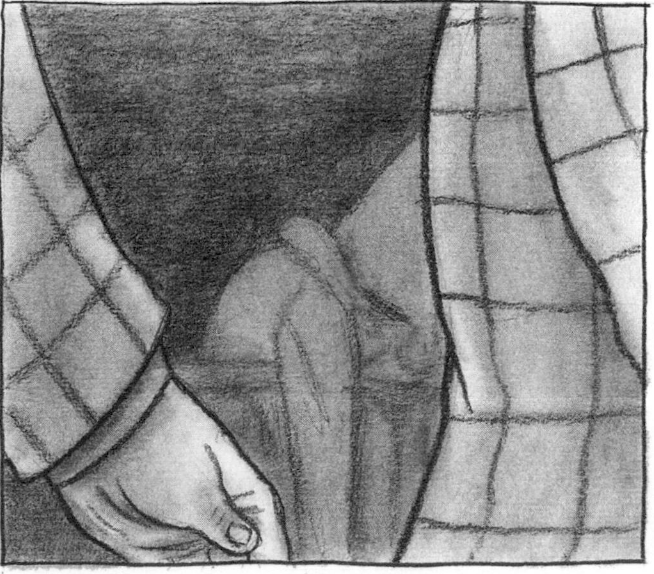

BAKERY

VAULT 4
VAULT 6

INVENTORY

?

??!

LISTEN...
THE WHOLE CITY'S GONE QUIET.

!!

VIOLET WAS RIGHT...

PPFFFT

THEY'RE KILLING EACH OTHER.

WE NEED TO LEAVE *NOW*. HOW DID YOU GET INTO THE CITY?
THE HARBOR.
I KNOW THE QUICK WAY THERE.

YOU'RE VERY... UNASSUMING.
...
YOU NEVER TOLD ME WHERE YOU COME FROM...

YOU... ACT AS IF YOU'VE SEEN A LOT... *HAVE* YOU?

I... BELIEVE WE'VE SEEN MOST EVERYTHING...
"*WE'VE*"? WHO'S *WE*?

AHHHCHOOO!

THAT'S MR. PIT...
WHO?

I MET HIM IN THE BAKERY...

THE MOON MAKES HIM SNEEZE...

SO HE AVOIDS THE OUTDOORS.

WHY WOULD HE--

AHHH CHOO

AAHHCHOOO

AAAHHHH

AHHHHCHOOO

MR. PIT!

GO, DEAR! THIS IS A TRAP!

WHO DID THIS TO YOU?

GET YOUR HANDS OFF MY SCARF.

WHO DO YOU THINK YOU ARE?

I AM SOMEONE WHO CARES FOR YOUR DREAMS, IF YOU WOULD HAVE THEM...

? ? ? ? ?

YOU ARE CHAOS! YOU HAVE TAKEN EVERYTHING FROM ME!!

YOU AND YOUR CHARMED LIFE...
??

!
YOU KNOW NOTHING ABOUT THE REAL WORLD!

YOU KNOW NOTHING ABOUT IMPOSSIBLE CHOICES!

DON'T LISTEN TO HIM!

HE'S JUST REPEATING WHAT I SAID WHEN THEY CAPTURED ME!
AH CHOO
AH CHOO

LEAVE THE OLD MAN OR I'LL BREAK THE CAT'S NECK.
NO.

NO!
I LOVE THEM BOTH...

PSSST! USE ME-- USE ME!

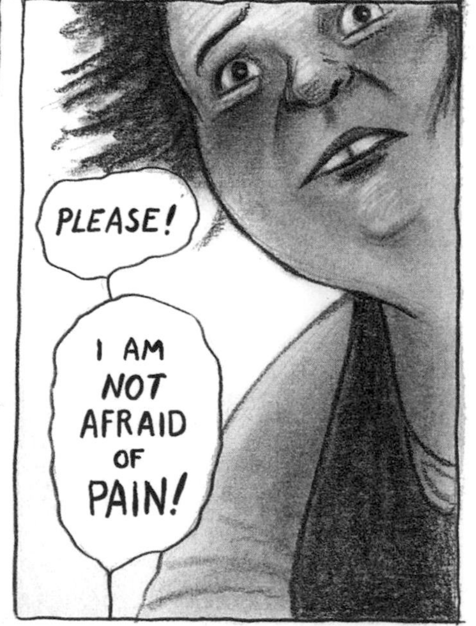
PLEASE!
I AM NOT AFRAID OF PAIN!

AHCHOO

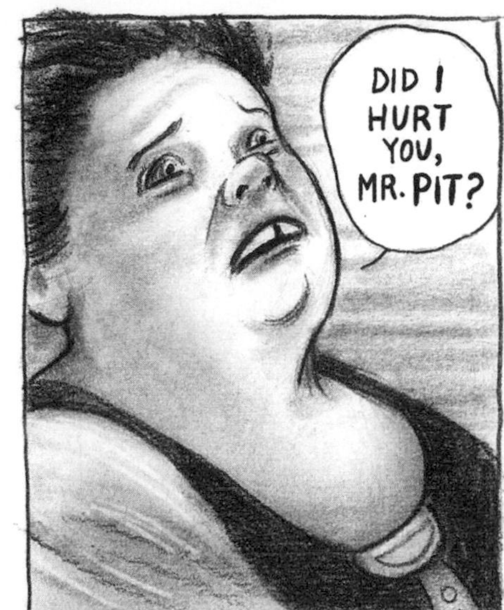
DID I HURT YOU, MR. PIT?

NOT AT ALL!

I'M STRONGER THAN I LOOK!

MR. PIT, THIS IS BETTY.
OH--HELLO, BETTY.
HOW DO YOU DO! TURN LEFT AT THE NEXT ALLEY...

IS HE STILL THERE?
YES.

MR. PIT, WOULD YOU LIKE TO TRAVEL WITH US?
YES! IF IT'S NO BOTHER.
NOT AT ALL.

NEWS
AAHHCHOO
WE WOULD LOVE TO HAVE YOU...

WHERE ARE WE GOING?

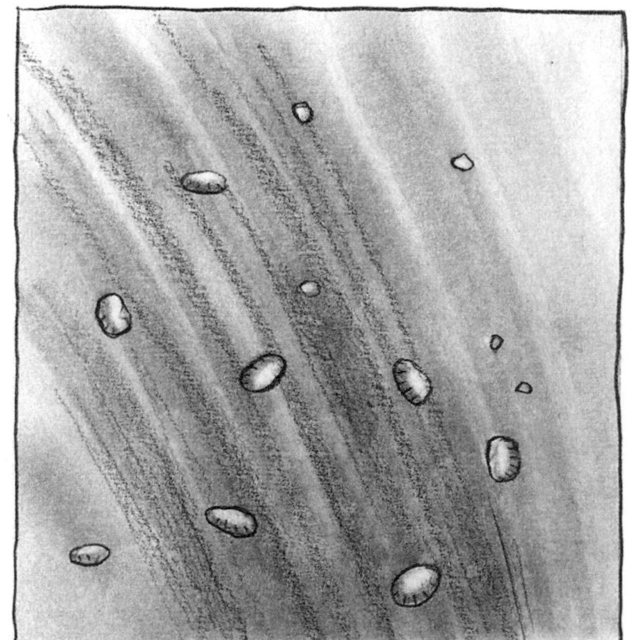

LEAVE ME ALONE WITH HER. SHE CAN'T SAVE YOU ANYMORE.
COWARD! WE ARE NOT LEAVING HER!

LEAVE ME TO DO WHAT I WANT!!

NEVER! WE WON'T ALLOW IT!!

YOU WON'T ALLOW IT?!! YOU ARE NOTHING! MEANINGLESS!
?!

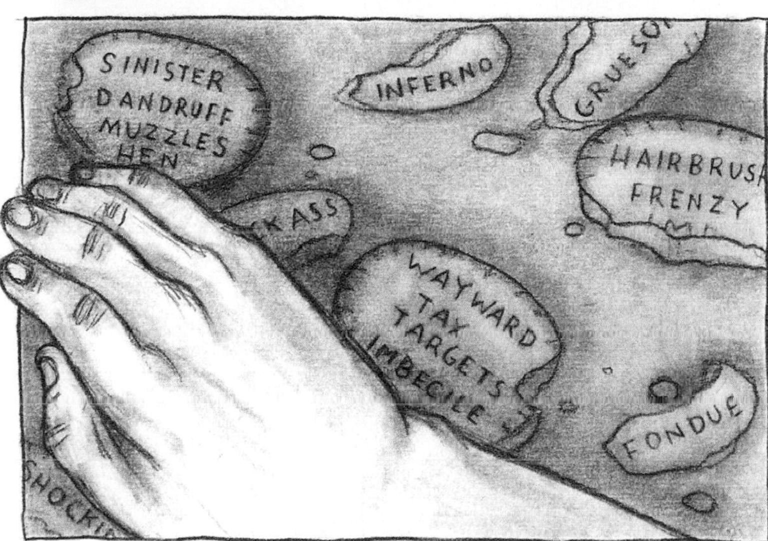
SINISTER DANDRUFF MUZZLES HEN
INFERNO
GRUESO
HAIRBRUS FRENZY
KASS
WAYWARD TAX TARGETS IMBECILE
FONDUE
SHOCKI

HA.
?

MEANINGLESS...
THEY'RE MEANING... LESS...
?

THE... BISCUITS... ARE... MEANINGLESS...
??

WHAT?

YOU ARE FILTHY-- RUINOUS!!
THAT IS ENOUGH!

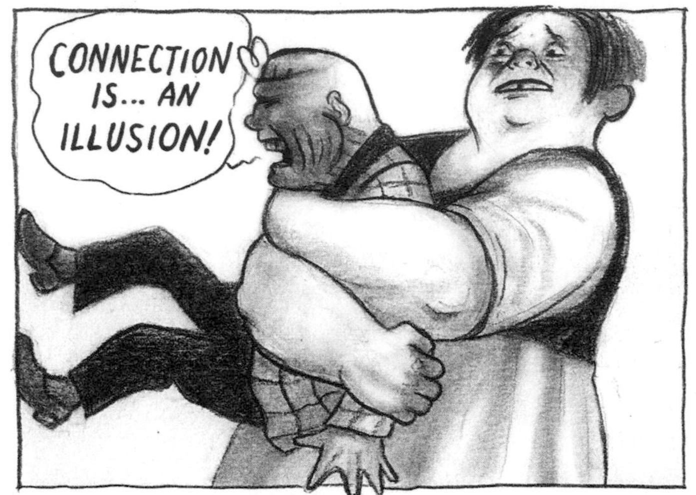
CONNECTION IS... AN ILLUSION!

MEANING IS A PHANTOM CONNECTION IS AN ILLUSION MEANING IS A PHANTOM

...I...WILL NEVER...TOUCH HER AGAIN, I...WILL...MEANING IS...A PHANTOM...CONNECTION...IS...AN...
...AN... ILLUSION.

MATTER IS...ALL.

...THAT MATTERS..
ZZZZ

ZZZ

ZZZZ
YOU COULD'VE KILLED HIM, BUT YOU DIDN'T.

IT'S BETTER THAT HE DREAMS.
ZZZ

HE'LL WAKE UP TO A NEW CITY...

...WHERE NOBODY WILL SEE HIM.

AH,
AH-
THE HARBOR!
THAT'S RIGHT.

LOOK-- THE BRIGHT MOON AND I'M NOT SNEEZING!
YES, MR. PIT.
AH...AH

AMAZING!

SO...THIS IS IT...

OH-- LOOK!

THE CITY IS SO SMALL FROM HERE!
YES.

AH..!

AAHHHCHOoooo

FOUND

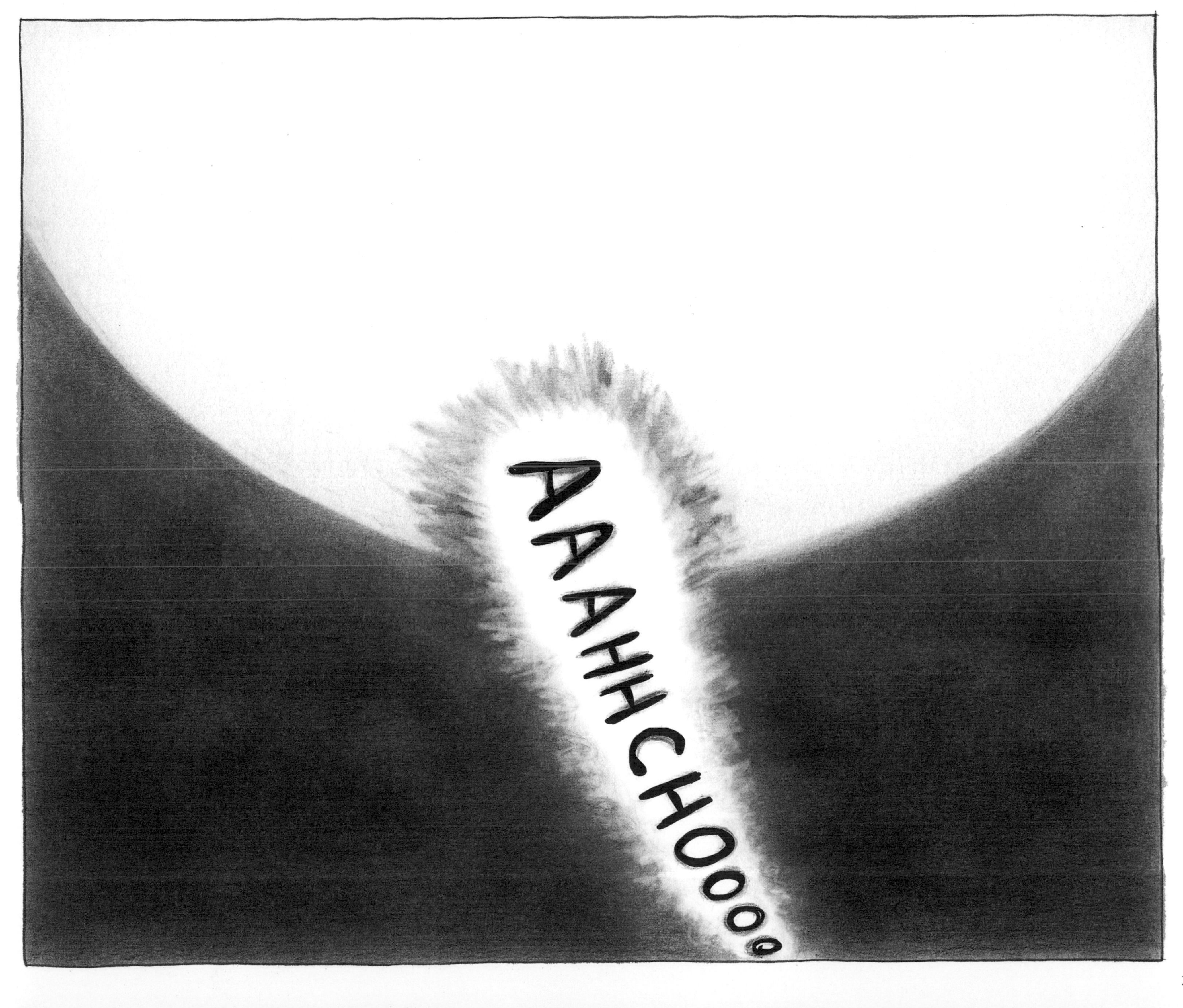
AAAHHCHOooo

IT'S TOO BIG...

IT'S GOING TO CRASH...
AND WE'LL ALL BE THROWN INTO SPACE...

AAAHH
AH AHHH CHOO
AH
IT'S TOO HEAVY WITH... LIGHT
MR. PIT, TRY LOOKING AT THE WATER..

LOOK--LOOK! IT'S FALLING!

GONE...
GONE
WE'LL ALL BE SCATTERED... ALONE NEVER TO RETURN..
ALONE..

SO MANY WAVES... HOW DO I ARRANGE THEM? THEY KEEP... KEEP COMING! SO.. SO... MANY.

AHHHHH
CHOOO

INFINITUDE...

...EXHAUSTS ME...

ZZZZZZZZ

DO YOU KNOW WHERE WE'RE GOING?

I KNOW THE **PLACE**, BUT NOT HOW TO GET THERE.

WILL THERE BE FLEAS?

DOGS?

?

ZZZZZ
?

MR. PIT IS RIGHT... THE MOON HERE IS SO...BIG. IT'S NOT LIKE OURS...
HAVE YOU GONE MAD?

DID I CHOOSE THE WRONG COMPANION?

NO, BETTY. WE ARE WELL-SUITED.

PRRRRR

VIOLET AND I TRAVELED ALL OVER THIS WORLD.

BUT THAT CITY! AFTER ONE WEEK I COULD FEEL IT TURNING ME ROTTEN.

THEN YOU CAME ALONG...
ANYWAY... OUT HERE THINGS ARE CLEAN.

NONE OF THAT SHAMING AND STEALING AND BRIBERY AND MURDER...

OH-- MY HOME HAS ALL THAT, TOO...

A LOT OF THE CITY GOES THERE, BUT IT PASSES THROUGH...
???

I WISH I'D GOTTEN THOSE SMOKE STICKS. NOW OLD LLOYD WILL DIE.
WHAT? NO, LISTEN..
ZZZZZ

AAAAAAAH CHOOOOOO!

THE MOON IS... IS CRASHING!

AM I DEAD? WHERE IS MY BODY?

OH... I'M TERRIBLY SORRY...

PRRR...

PRRRRR
PRRR

THANK YOU... FOR CALMING ME.
NOT AT ALL. IT'S MY JOB.
PRRR

WHAT HAPPENED TO YOU, MR. PIT, WITH THE MOON?

I'VE... NEVER TOLD ANYONE...
PRRRRR

...BUT I'LL TELL YOU.
PRRRR

THE YOUNG DON'T KNOW DREAMS FROM REAL THINGS, AND THAT IS GOOD...
...BUT I WAS NOT SO YOUNG...

I SAW THINGS AS THEY WERE, NOT AS I WISHED THEY COULD BE. IN THAT WAY I WAS LIKE MY MOTHER.

I WISH YOU WOULD BELIEVE ME!
IT... JUST DOESN'T MAKE SENSE.

ARE WE EXPECTED TO PRODUCE LESS, JUST TO APPEASE THEM?
I DON'T KNOW, BUT THEY'RE STARTING TO SHUN US.

FATHER WAS AN IDEALIST WHO FED ON HIS OWN LOGIC. MOTHER ALWAYS HAD TO WORK HARD TO SHOW HIM THE SENSE OF THINGS.

THIS MORNING AT MARKET THEY ASKED ME WHERE I'D GOTTEN MY HAT PIN. THEY *KNOW* IT'S BEEN IN THE FAMILY FOR THREE GENERATIONS! THEY'RE STARTING TO TURN US INTO STRANGERS...

YOU KNOW WHAT THAT *MEANS!* THE ARMY WILL USE THE OTHER VILLAGES TO DESTROY *OURS*.

WHAT ARE WE TO *DO?* WE CAN'T SIMPLY *LEAVE!*
WHY *NOT?* WE'LL TAKE THE CHILDREN TO A BETTER PLACE--A *NEW START*...

I'M *NOT LEAVING* THIS LAND! MY FAMILY SETTLED IT LONG BEFORE THOSE OTHERS!

LISTEN:
NONE OF THAT MATTERS NOW. THE MOB *WILL COME*, AND EVERYONE IN IT WILL FEEL STRONG AND BLAMELESS...
WE *CAN'T STAY HERE*.

YOU AND DADDY FIGHTING?
NO, NO..

WE'RE OUT OF PLUMS. GO UP TO THE FOREST AND PICK US SOME. TAKE THE LITTLE ONES ALONG.

PICK EVERY LAST ONE, Y'HEAR?
YES, MA'AM!

HA.

WE LOVED OUR CHORE.

HA!

THE PLUMS WERE MAGICAL. THEY MADE TIME DISAPPEAR. AND THE PITS?! EACH WAS MORE PERFECT THAN THE LAST.

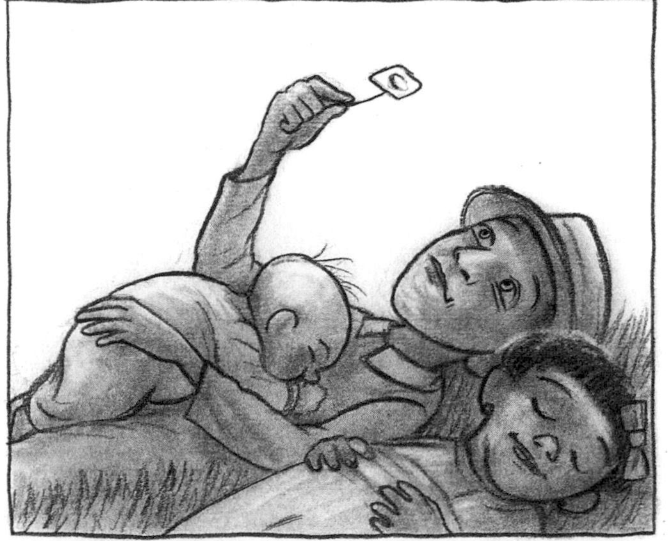

MAMA...
..PAPA..

EVERYONE I'D EVER KNOWN LAY IN FRONT OF ME, SILENT INSIDE A ROAR OF FLAMES.

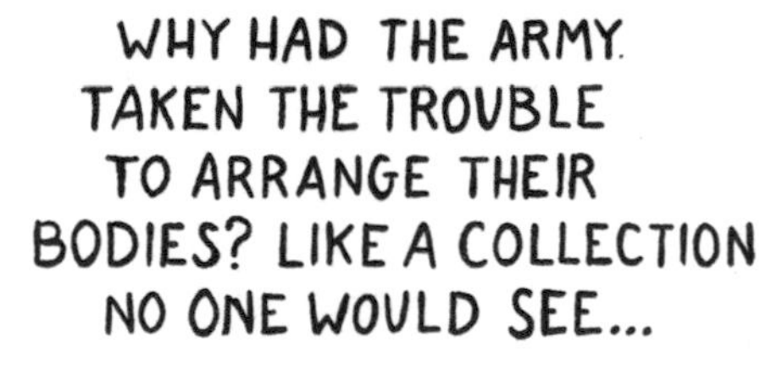
WHY HAD THE ARMY TAKEN THE TROUBLE TO ARRANGE THEIR BODIES? LIKE A COLLECTION NO ONE WOULD SEE...

I DIDN'T WANT TO BELIEVE IT...
I DIDN'T WANT TO BELIEVE *ANYTHING*.

I WISHED I'D NEVER HAD EYES TO SEE...
...HOW CHAOS HAD SO SPITEFULLY ARRANGED EVERY FINALITY...

...BUT THEN SOME OF MY WORLD RETURNED.

I COULDN'T EVEN MUSTER THE STRENGTH FOR JOY.

I'M HUNGRY.
...THE WORLD SAID. IT WANTED TO GO HOME. AND THE REST OF THE WORLD
HA HA!
LAUGHED, AS IT ALWAYS HAD.

WE'D EATEN ALL THE FRUIT. THE FOREST HAD NOTHING LEFT TO GIVE...

...AND THROUGH THE TREES I COULD FEEL THE IMPLACABLE DARKNESS...

"YOUR SISTER IS YOUNG" THE DARKNESS WHISPERED, "SHE WILL FOLLOW YOU AND BELIEVE ANYTHING YOU SAY. SO CLOSE YOUR EYES AND LIE WELL. HOLD THE WORLD TOGETHER."

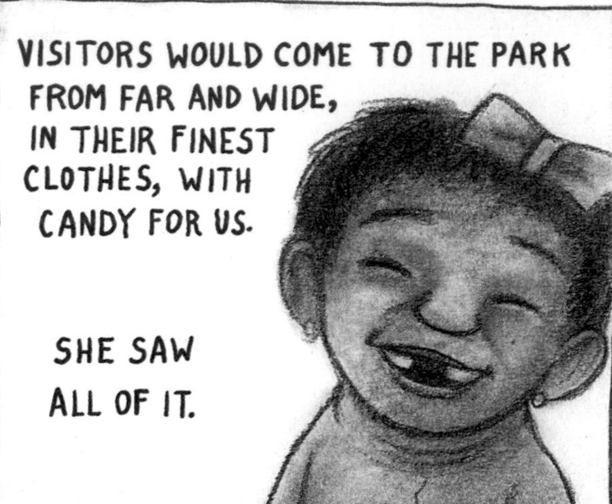

THEY'RE NOT FINISHED! YOU MUST LEAVE HERE.

GO!!

QUICKLY!

FOLLOW MY VOICE!
I DON'T KNOW WHAT IT WAS, BUT IT MOVED SWIFTLY, SILENTLY,
AND SPOKE TO US WITHOUT SPEAKING.
WE FOLLOWED IT THROUGH PLACES SO NARROW THAT ONLY THE MOMENT COULD GET THROUGH.

OUR FEET NEVER SEEMED TO TOUCH THE GROUND...
THIS WAY...
...AND WE DIDN'T NEED EYES TO SEE.

FOLLOW!

FOLLOW!
WE NEVER HAD TO LEAVE THE BEAUTIFUL PARK IN OUR DREAM.
EVEN THE BABY SEEMED TO SEE IT.

I DON'T REMEMBER HOW WE CROSSED THE BORDER, OR WHEN WE STOPPED HEARING THE VOICE.
I DON'T RECALL HOW WE GOT TO THE CITY, OR HOW LONG WE'D BEEN SLEEPING IN THAT DOORWAY.
ZZZ

I KNOW ONLY THAT OVERNIGHT I'D LEARNED THE SCENT OF MALEVOLENCE.
ZZZ

EVEN IN MY SLEEP I COULD SMELL IT...
ZZZ
ZZZ

...THE STENCH OF BUSY PEOPLE, DECIDING WHO WAS USEFUL AND WHO WAS IN THE WAY.
ZZZ

DAMMIT..
WORKHOUSE

GO AROUND.!

I HAD LEARNED HOW TO LOSE...

YES, MA'AM.

...AND I HAD LEARNED HOW TO LIE.
THAT'S OUR AUNTIE. GO TELL HER ABOUT THE MOON.

I RECOGNIZED PEOPLE WHO WOULD UNDERSTAND...

...PEOPLE OF INNATE SYMPATHIES...
!!?!!

SHE UNDERSTOOD OUR STORY EXACTLY...
THE MOON FELL AND SAID "FOLLOW"?...
IT MOVED HER.

...AND THE WORLD DISAPPEARED, DID IT?
SHE KNEW THE DIALECT, THE DIRT IN THE CLOTHES, THE SMELL OF WAR ON MY SISTER...

YOU HAVE A CHOICE TO FORGET ALL THAT. LIVE WITH US AND YOU'LL BE FREE.

I'VE BEEN UP IN THE CEMETERY, SENDING DOWN DISPATCHES.
BUT THAT'S DONE. THE WAR ENDED THIS MORNING.

AND NOW WE'LL HAVE A BIG ANTENNA...

...AND MORE MONEY THAN WE'D EVER IMAGINED... FROM BISCUITS..!

WHAT'S THIS?

IT'S SO BEAUTIFUL...

WHY--THAT'S A PIT, ISN'T IT?

I'LL TAKE IT TO THE JEWELER AND MAKE YOU A NICE BROOCH.

IF SHE'D SEEN WHAT I'D SEEN MY SISTER WOULD HAVE DIED. SO I LEFT HER WITH A PIT FROM HOME AND A BRIGHT, HAPPY PLACE BEHIND HER EYES.

I COULDN'T LET HER GROW UP SEEING THE HORROR IN MINE.
SHE WOULD FORGET ME, AND THAT WAS GOOD.

I'VE ASKED MYSELF MANY TIMES, WHY DID THAT WAR HAPPEN?
THERE MUST'VE BEEN A GOOD REASON..

...BUT I ALWAYS GIVE MYSELF THE SAME ANSWER...

SOMEONE DECIDED THAT SOMEONE ELSE WAS IN THE WAY.

IN THE WAY OF WHAT? NOTHING THEY COULDN'T HAVE GOTTEN BY GOING AROUND.

THE WAR WASN'T ABOUT LAND OR GOODS OR CREEDS...

IT WAS ABOUT PUSHING SOMEONE ELSE ASIDE.

OH, MR. PIT..

YOUR SISTER'S NAME IS VIOLET, AND I KNOW HER!

DO YOU?!
YES!

WE'VE BEEN COMPANIONS FOR YEARS!

I'M SORRY IF SHE FORGOT YOU. THE TWO OF YOU WOULD'VE GOTTEN ON WELL.

WAS SHE GOOD TO YOU?
OH YES.

VIOLET IS GOOD TO EVERYONE.

MR. PIT...

WHAT HAPPENED TO THE BABY?

YOU HAVE TO UNDERSTAND...

I'D USED A LIFETIME OF COURAGE IN TWO DAYS.

FROM THEN ON EVERYTHING FRIGHTENED ME, AND I WAS TIRED OF RUNNING.

AAAHCHOO.
HA!
THAT NIGHT I TOOK US UP HIGH ABOVE THE HARBOR. I WAS GOING TO JUMP WITH THE BABY...

AHHHCHOOO!
?
...WHEN A STRANGE OLD MAN IN A POINTED HAT APPEARED...

"AH CHOO"? WHAT THE HELL IS *THAT* SUPPOSED TO MEAN??
SMOKE STICKS

AHHCHOOOo
HA!
LET ME GUESS--YOU WANT ANOTHER "EXPORT TAX" BEFORE YOU LET ME OUTA THIS HELL HOLE?

WAIT-- YOU'RE JUST A KID-- WITH A BABY!

TAKE THE STAIRS DOWN HERE NOW!
Y--YESSIR.

WHAT WERE YOU PLANNING TO DO UP THERE?

TH-- THE M-MOON... IT...F--FELL... TO... THE GROUND AND T--TOLD US... TO.. GO..

AND YOU THOUGHT YOU'D ESCAPE IT BY JUMPING TO YOUR DEATH...

LISTEN TO ME...

WHERE I COME FROM WE HAVE A SPECIAL BRIDGE. IT ATTRACTS CERTAIN TYPES-- CALL THEM "DREAMS."

THEY DON'T GO THERE TO JUMP OFF THAT BRIDGE. THEY GO THERE TO JUMP BACK ON, TRYING TO TAKE BACK THE LAST MISTAKE OF THEIR LIVES...

THEY LIE ON THE GROUND BELOW AND LET THEMSELVES FLY BACK UP TO THE SPOT WHERE THEY'D JUMPED.

DO YOU KNOW WHAT AN ARCHIVE IS?
Y--YES, SIR...

WELL, I WORK IN ONE. I'VE HAD TO FILE AWAY MORE THAN MY SHARE OF PEOPLE'S LAST-MOMENT REGRETS. WE ARE RUNNING OUT OF SHELVES, KID.

Y--YOU'RE NOT FROM HERE, SIR?
THIS DUMP?! 'COURSE NOT.

THEN... TAKE HER, TAKE HER, PLEASE!
HELL, NO!!
HA!

ANOTHER TRICK! YOU CITY FOLK TAKE US FOR FOOLS!

I MAY COME FROM NOWHERE, BUT BELIEVE ME, I'VE SEEN IT ALL!

SONOFASONOFA SONOFABITCH! ALL I WANTED WERE SMOKE STICKS!!
HA!

HA HA HA HA!

WHAT'S SO FUNNY?

TAKE HER, SIR!
I WON'T BE MADE A FOOL!
HA!
PLEASE..

TAKE HER OR I'LL DROP HER!!

ALL RIGHT, ALREADY!
WAIT!
WAIT...

SONOFASONOFA SONOFABITCH...

DAMMIT, GIVE ME THAT!

NOW YOU LISTEN TO ME: WHATEVER HAPPENED TO YOU, THERE'LL COME A TIME WHEN YOU'LL DREAM AGAIN.

YOU HAVE TO ALLOW FOR THAT! DREAMING IS WHAT YOU'RE SUPPOSED TO DO, UNDERSTAND?

W--WHERE WILL YOU TAKE HER?

I'M GOING BACK TO A PLACE NO ONE HERE CAN FIND, BECAUSE THEY DON'T BELIEVE IT EXISTS.

I LIVE WHERE DREAMS LIVE. SO IF YOU WANT TO CONTACT HER YOU'LL HAVE TO SEND YOUR DREAMS. DON'T SCARE HER! DELIGHT HER. SHE'LL FIND THEM.

UNLESS, OF COURSE, YOU'D LIKE TO COME WITH US.

AAAAAAHHCHOOOOO!
SONOFABITCH...
HA!

I'LL BE BACK FOR YOU, KID.

HA, HA..
LOOK AT THAT..

HE SENT YOU OFF WITH A SEED...
...FROM HOME.

IN THE FJORD WE CALL THIS AN "EXILE'S SUITCASE."

I'LL PLANT IT FOR YOU SOMEPLACE NICE.

YOU SHOULD KNOW THAT I FIND MOST PEOPLE IRRITATING...
HA HA HA!
HE SAID HE LIVED WHERE DREAMS LIVED. IT SOUNDED LIKE A FAIRY TALE, BUT I DECIDED TO BELIEVE IT.

I WENT BACK INTO THE CITY. THE WORKHOUSE RUSTLERS CAUGHT ME, BUT I WAS TOO WEAK FOR HARD LABOR. THE BAKERY KINDLY TOOK ME IN, AND THERE I STAYED.
NOW AND THEN MRS. BISCUIT WOULD BRING HER NEW DAUGHTER TO THE BAKERY. I WOULD ALWAYS RUN AND HIDE. I THINK SHE REALIZED THAT WE WERE SIBLINGS. SHE RESPECTED MY WISHES AND LET ME BE.
YEARS PASSED AND I WORKED MY WAY UP TO THE INVENTORY ROOM. I WAS HAPPY THERE, ARRANGING OTHER PEOPLE'S THINGS. I'D BROUGHT MY OWN SEED FROM HOME AND PLANTED IT. IT GREW INTO A TREE.
?!

AND EVERY NIGHT I'D SEND MY DREAMS TO THE BABY, JUST AS THE OLD MAN SAID TO DO.

I'D MAKE MYSELF TALL AND DAPPER AND ADVENTUROUS. I WOULD FLY, OR JUGGLE MOUNTAINS, OR MAKE THE WIND INTO MY ORCHESTRA...

...ANYTHING THAT MIGHT MAKE THE BABY LAUGH, WHEREVER SHE WAS.

EVENTUALLY I STOPPED SENDING DREAMS, BECAUSE I STOPPED HAVING THEM...

...BUT IF I COULDN'T DREAM I COULD AT LEAST *LIVE*, AND BELIEVE THE THINGS THAT BROUGHT ME JOY.

PRRRR

OH, THE SOUND OF THE BABY'S LAUGHTER...

I REMEMBER IT SO CLEARLY...

WHAT DID SHE FIND SO *FUNNY?*

EVERYTHING, APPARENTLY...

HE TRICKED ME!
OLD LLOYD...

HE ALWAYS SAYS THAT MY MOTHER FINDS EVERYTHING FUNNY...

...AND... MAMA WORKS UNDER A TREE...

...THAT IS JUST LIKE YOURS!

?!

OLD LLOYD ALWAYS CALLS MAMA HIS "CITY GIRL."

"SMOKE STICKS," HA!

HE KNEW I WOULD FIND YOU.

!!???
HA!!!

LOOK!

THAT'S OUR MOON!

WHAT ARE THOSE?

THOSE ARE DREAMS.!

SO... THE OLD MAN WAS SPEAKING TRUTH...
YES! OLD LLOYD LIES ONLY WHEN HE NEEDS TO.

JUST HOW OLD IS HE? HE WAS VERY OLD SO LONG AGO...
OLD LLOYD? WELL, HMMM...
HEY...

I SAID HEY!!

WE'RE HOME!

OLD LLOYD?

OLD LLOYD?

WHY ARE YOU YELLING?

I CAN HEAR YOU JUST FINE.

WHAT TOOK YOU SO LONG?

YOU BRING ME SMOKE STICKS?
NO, OLD LLOYD.

GOOD. I HATE THOSE THINGS. THEY SHORTEN YOUR LIFE.

HHMPH..

I SAID I'D COME BACK FOR YOU, AND I DID, MORE TIMES THAN I CAN COUNT.

I WOULD'VE GIVEN UP IF YOU HADN'T KEPT SENDING YOUR DREAMS. YOUR SISTER SAW EVERY ONE OF THEM.

MY SISTER--*THE* BABY?
YEAH, YEAH--SSSHHH! DON'T INTERRUPT...

YEARS AGO, WHEN YOU STOPPED SENDING DREAMS, I THOUGHT THAT WAS THE END OF YOU. THEN THIS MORNING A DREAM CAME IN ABOUT A FALLING MOON, AND I KNEW YOU WERE STILL THERE...

...SO I SENT EARTHA HERE TO FETCH YOU, BECAUSE SHE GETS INTO ALL THE RIGHT KINDS OF TROUBLE.

ALL RIGHT, ALL RIGHT-- YOU'RE SQUEEZING TOO HARD...

ENOUGH ALREADY WITH THE AFFECTION!
OH EARTHA, THANK GOODNESS YOUR'E BACK!

LLOYD'S BEEN A NERVOUS WRECK ALL DAY.

YOU KNOW WHERE I'VE BEEN?
OF COURSE!

WE'VE ALWAYS KNOWN EVERYTHING, BUT WE KEEP SECRETS SAFE HERE.

ALL RIGHT, NO MORE AFTER THIS, I MEAN IT!

AND THIS?? HHHRMPH!!!

GET THIS GUY TO THE BARBER.

I HOPE YOU'RE A GOOD WORKER, YOUNG FELLA...

ARCHIVE
...BECAUSE THE ARCHIVE IS ABOUT TO GET *VERY* BUSY.

NOW GET OUTA HERE!

PRRRRR

HOW ARE YOU WITH VERMIN?
PRRRRR

THAT MOON DREAM--WHO SENT IT HERE ?

YOUR SISTER VIOLET.
OH...

I DON'T THINK SHE *EVER* FORGOT YOU, UNCLE PIT.

MAYBELLE!

EARTHA!

I'VE BEEN LOOKING EVERYWHERE FOR YOU! YOU'LL NEVER GUESS WHAT'S HAPPENED...

THOUSANDS OF DREAMS-- *EVERYWHERE!*

ALL OF A SUDDEN THEY SPROUTED IN THE FIELDS!

ISN'T IT *GRAND?* THE CITY FOLK ARE *DREAMING* AGAIN!!

I MISSED YOU TODAY...

...BUT REST DID YOU GOOD.

YOU FEEL LIKE YOU'VE LET THE WHOLE WORLD IN...

For hours Eartha could do nothing but cry.
She had so much to tell Maybelle, but her tongue stumbled. Maybelle knew that in time a story would come.
It was up to Pit to introduce himself, much to Maybelle's surprise; she thought she knew everyone in Echo Fjord...
!!!

?.
THESE ARE DREAMS?
AYE.

AND... MY DREAMS CAME HERE?!

SOB
SOB
??!

HA, HA!

MAMA, PAPA!
DARLING GIRL! HA HA HA... ALL RESTED?
OH--SWEET CHILD!

!!!
YOU MISSED ALL THE THRILL!
WHAT A DAY WE'VE HAD!

!!!
AND WHO'S THIS DASHING LAD?
WELL, WELL! WE THOUGHT WE KNEW *EVERY SOUL* IN THIS FJORD!

LOOK ATCHA! YOU'VE EITHER *BEEN* TO THE PUB...
...OR YOU'RE IN DIRE NEED OF GOING!
!!!
HA HA HA HA...

YOU COMIN', EARTHA?
MAYBE LATER, MAMA..

ZZZ
ARCHIVE
ZZ
YOU'VE BEEN TO THE CITY AND BACK? SINCE THIS *MORNING?!* HOW CAN THAT *BE?*
I DON'T KNOW, BUT HERE WE ARE...
DOES YOUR MA KNOW HE'S HER BROTHER?
HE'LL TELL HER SOON, I'M SURE.

I LOVE YOU, MAYBELLE.
I KNOW.
IT'S GOOD TO BE HOME.
ZZZZ
ZZZZ

Old Lloyd finally took a sound nap, knowing there would be many more stories to tell, and many Dreams to help along their way.
Echo Fjord would keep to its ancient oath: to guide the Dreams and leave the City dreamers be.
ZZZZ
ZZZZ

ZZZ
ZZZ

ZZZ
ZZZ
ZZZ

ZZ
ZZ

SO, WORLD TRAVELER, MAYBE ONE DAY I'LL TELL YOU THE STORY...

...OF A LONG-AGO TIME, WHEN A FELLA LOST HIS FIRST WIFE...

...AND FIGURED "WHAT'S THE USE?", SO HE GOT ON A BOAT AND HOPED THE SEA WOULD SWALLOW HIM, BUT IT WOULDN'T, BECAUSE HE WAS TOO BITTER...

...SO IT SPAT HIM ALL THE WAY TO THE CITY, A PLACE RIFE WITH LITTLE HELLS.

UNDETERRED, HE TRADED TURNIPS FOR A CRATE OF SMOKE STICKS, AND SET OFF TO SMOKE HIMSELF TO DEATH ON THE WAVES...

...BUT THEN HE HEARD A BOY SNEEZE, AND A BABY LAUGH...
...AND SUDDENLY THE WORLD BECAME REAL AGAIN...
ZZZ
ZZZ

SUDDENLY...EVERYTHING MATTERED.
ZZZ
ZZZ